A-Z CANTERBURY MARGATE and RAM

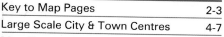

G000278923

CONTENTS

Key to Map Pages	2-3
Large Scale City & Town Centres	4-7
Map Pages	8-48

Index to
Villages,
and sele

Guide to

REFERENCE

Motorway	**M2**
A Road	**A28**
Tunnel	
B Road	**B2052**
Dual Carriageway	
One-way Street Traffic flow on A roads is also indicated by a heavy line on the driver's left.	
Road Under Construction Opening dates are correct at the time of publication	
Proposed Road	
Restricted Access	
Pedestrianized Road	
Track & Footpath	
Residential Walkway	
Railway Level Crossing Station Tunnel	
Built-up Area EAST LA	
Local Authority Boundary	
Posttown Boundary	
Postcode Boundary (within Posttown)	
Map Continuation **8** Large Scale City Centre **4**	
Airport	✈

Car Park (selected)	P
Church or Chapel	†
City Wall (large scale only)	⅄⅄⅄⅄
Cycleway (selected)	🚲
Fire Station	■
Hospital	H
House Numbers (A & B Roads only)	48 113
Information Centre	i
National Grid Reference	⁶30
Park & Ride	Wincheap **P+R**
Police Station	▲
Post Office	★
Safety Camera with Speed Limit Fixed cameras and long term road works cameras. Symbols do not indicate camera direction.	(30)
Toilet: with facilities for the Disabled without facilities for the Disabled	▽ ▽
Educational Establishment	▢
Hospital or Healthcare Building	▢
Industrial Building	▢
Leisure or Recreational Facility	▢
Place of Interest	▢
Public Building	▢
Shopping Centre & Market	▢
Other Selected Buildings	▢

SCALE

Large Scale Pages 4-5 (Canterbury)
1:3,960 16 inches (40.64 cm) to 1 mile 25.4 cm to 1 km
0 1/16 ⅛ Mile

Large Scale Pages 6-7 (Margate & Ramsgate)
1:7,920 8 inches (20.32cm) to 1 mile 12.63cm to 1km
0 ⅛ ¼ Mile

0 50 100 150 Metres
0 100 200 300 Metres

Map Pages 8-48
1:15,840 4 inches (10.16cm) to 1 mile 6.31cm to 1km
0 ¼ ½ Mile

0 250 500 750 Metres 1 Kilometre

Copyright of Geographers' A-Z Map Company Limited

Fairfield Road, Borough Green, Sevenoaks, Kent TN15 8PP
Telephone: 01732 781000 (Enquiries & Trade Sales)
01732 783422 (Retail Sales)
www.az.co.uk
Copyright © Geographers' A-Z Map Co. Ltd.
Edition 4 2013

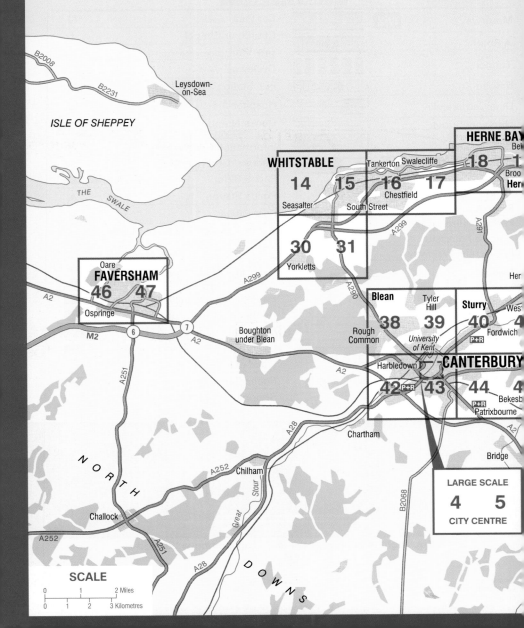

NORTH

B2008

B2231

Leysdown-on-Sea

ISLE OF SHEPPEY

THE SWALE

HERNE BAY

Bel

WHITSTABLE

Tankerton Swalecliffe

14 **15** **16** **17**

18 **1**

Broo

Her

Seasalter

South Street

Chestfield

A299

A291

30 **31**

Yorkletts

A290

Her

Oare

FAVERSHAM

46 **47**

Ospringe

A2

Blean

Tyler Hill

Sturry

Wes

38 **39**

40 **4**

M2

6

7

A2

Boughton
under Blean

Rough
Common

University
of Kent

P+R

Fordwich

A251

Harbledown

CANTERBURY

42 P+R

43

44 **4**

P+R

Bekesb

Patrixbourne

A2

Chartham

Bridge

B2068

NORTH

A28

A252

Chilham

Stour

Great Stour

LARGE SCALE

4 **5**

CITY CENTRE

Challock

A252

A251

A28

DOWNS

SCALE

0 — 1 — 2 Miles

0 — 1 — 2 — 3 Kilometres

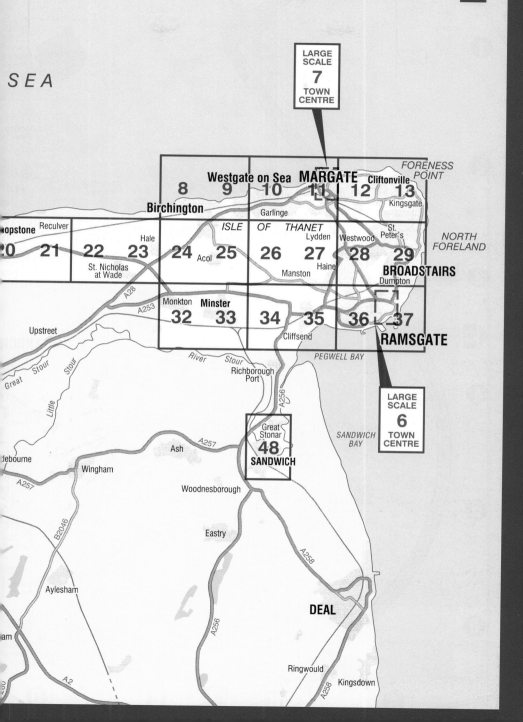

3

SEA

LARGE SCALE **7** TOWN CENTRE

FORENESS POINT

Westgate on Sea **MARGATE** Cliftonville

8 **9** **10** **11** **12** **13** Kingsgate

Birchington

Garlinge

opstone Reculver

ISLE OF THANET Lydden Westwood St. Peter's

NORTH FORELAND

20 **21** **22** **23** Hale **24** Acol **25** **26** **27** **28** **29**

St. Nicholas at Wade

Haine

Manston

BROADSTAIRS

Dumpton

Monkton **Minster**

32 **33** **34** **35** **36** **37**

Upstreet

Cliffsend

RAMSGATE

River Stour

Great Stour

Little Stour

Richborough Port

PEGWELL BAY

LARGE SCALE **6** TOWN CENTRE

Great Stonar **48** SANDWICH

SANDWICH BAY

lebourne

Ash

A257

Wingham

A257

Woodnesborough

B2046

Eastry

A258

Aylesham

am

A256

DEAL

A2

Ringwould

A258

Kingsdown

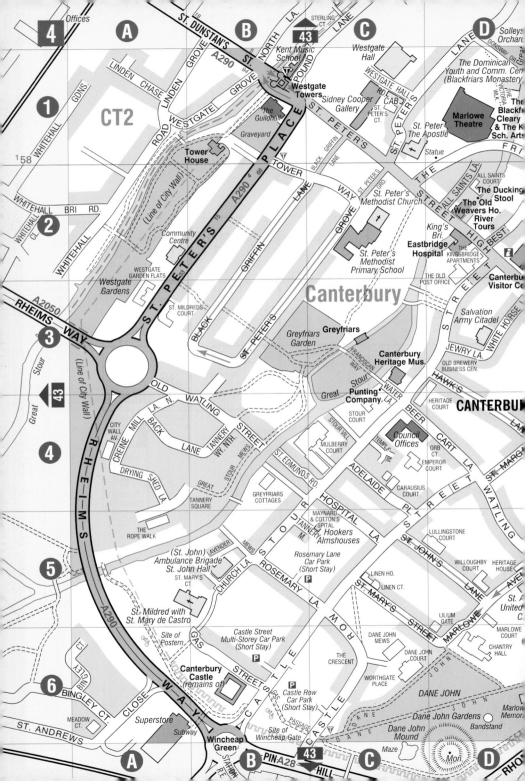

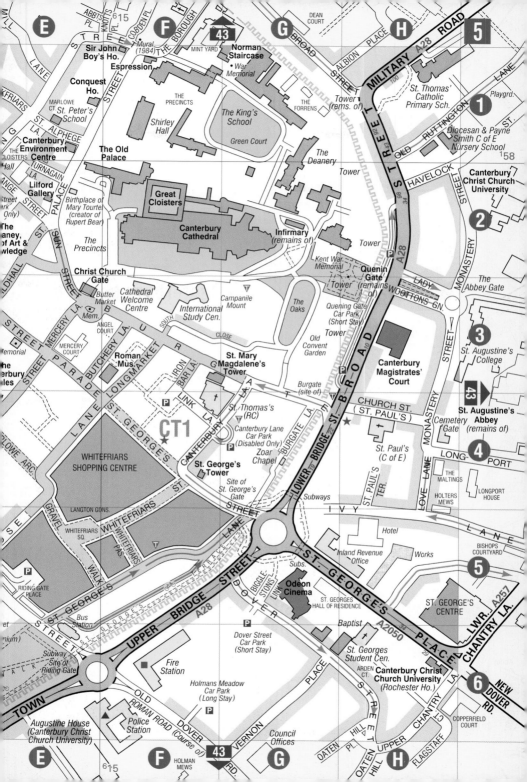

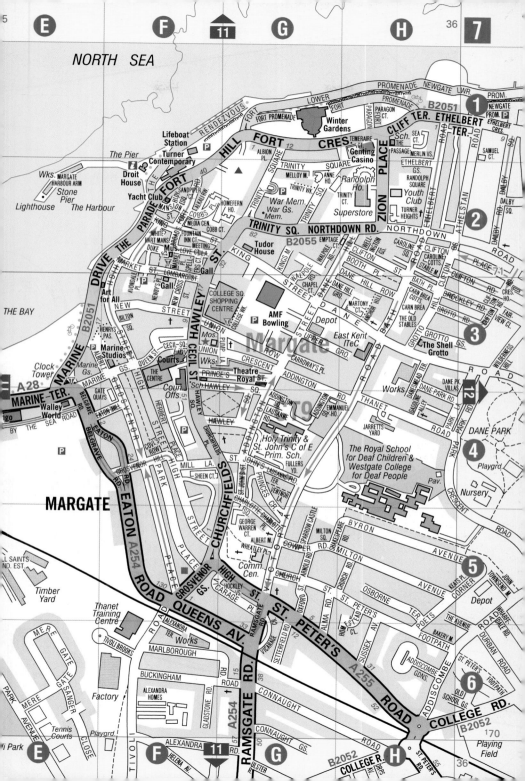

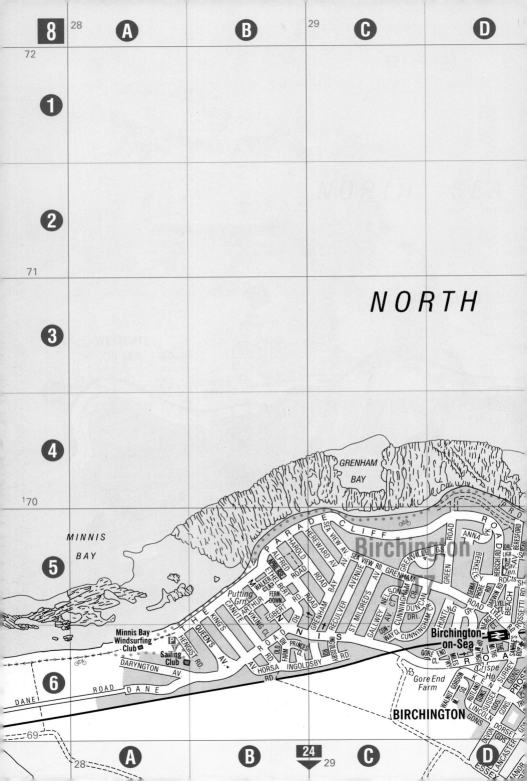

1

2

71

NORTH

3

4

GRENHAM BAY

170

MINNIS BAY

Birchington

5

PARADE

CLIFF

Putting Grn

Minnis Bay
Windsurfing
Club

Sailing
Club

DARYNGTON AV.

6

DANE

ROAD DANE

DANEI

69

Gore End
Farm

Gore End

Birchington-
on-Sea

BIRCHINGTON

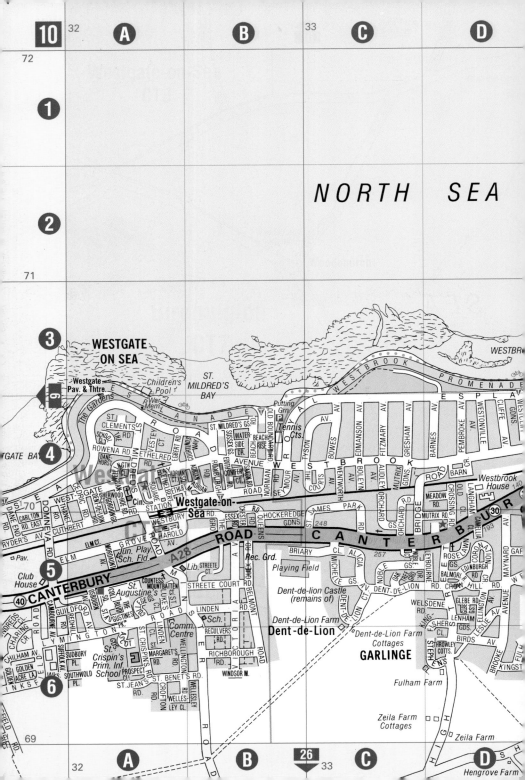

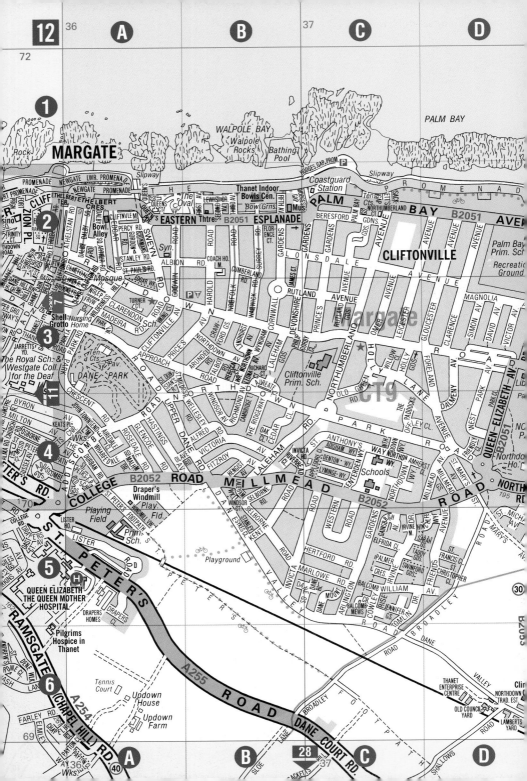

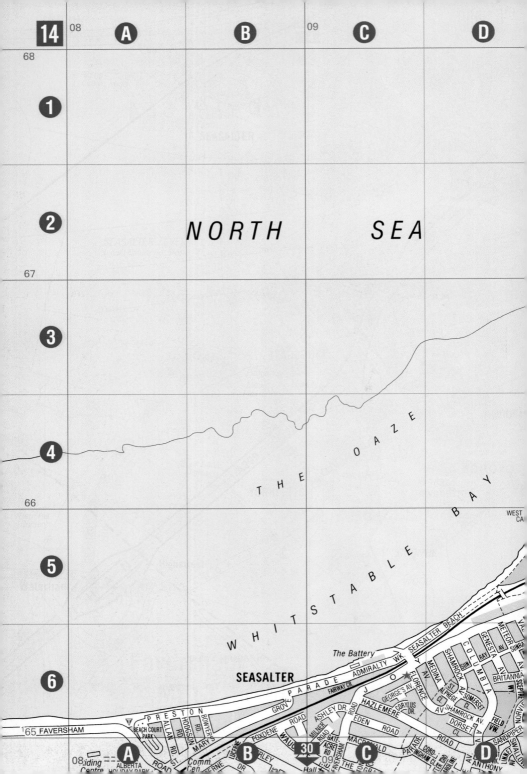

A   **B**   **C**   **D**

68

1

2

NORTH   *SEA*

67

3

T H E   O A Z E

4

66

WEST CA

5

W H I T S T A B L E   B A Y

The Battery

SEASALTER BEACH

SEASALTER

PARADE   FAIRWAY CR.   ADMIRALTY WK.

6

GROVE

George's AV.

COLUMBIA

METEOR

SUNR

SHAMROCK

GENESTA

BAY AV.

FLORENCE

MEDINA

BRITANNIA

W.

HAZLEMERE

CORYLUS DR.

ALPHEGE

SOMERSET CL.

FIELD

VW.

SHAMROCK AV.

ASHLEY DR.

EDEN   ROAD

DORSET CL.

SANDPIPER

65   FAVERSHAM

PRESTON

BEACH COURT PARK

ALBERTA

ROAD

ALLAN RD.

HODGSON RD.

BOWYERS RD.

MARY'S ST.

LUCERNE DR.

FOXDENE

WAUL

ILEY

MILNER

ROAD

MACDONALD

GATE

ACRE RD.

FAVERSHAM ROAD

PATTADE

CORD. CL

ER RD.

DOLINE

ROAD

ANTHONY

SWALLOW

A   **B**   **30**   **C**   **D**

Commit Cen

Hall

09

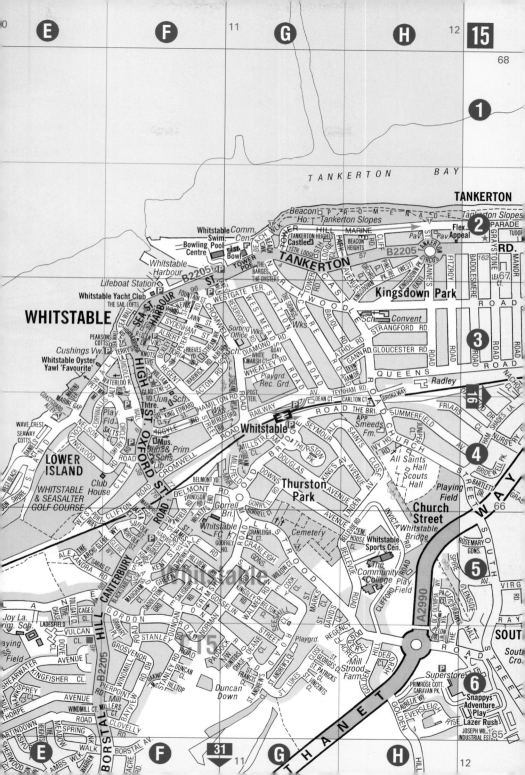

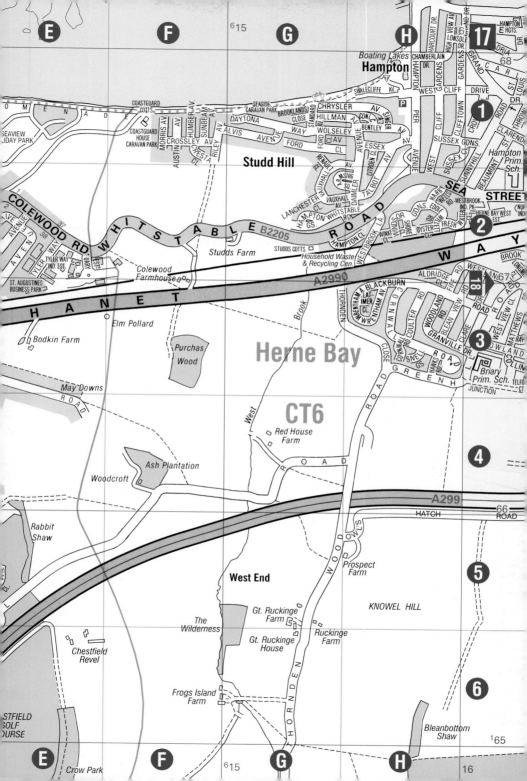

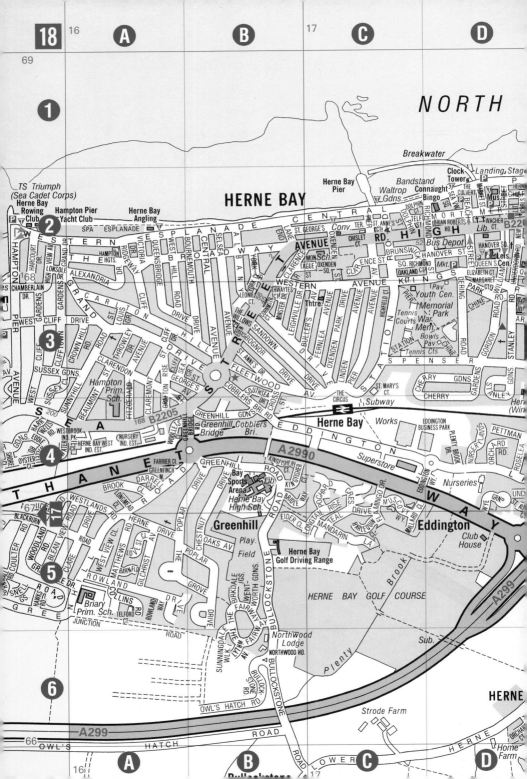

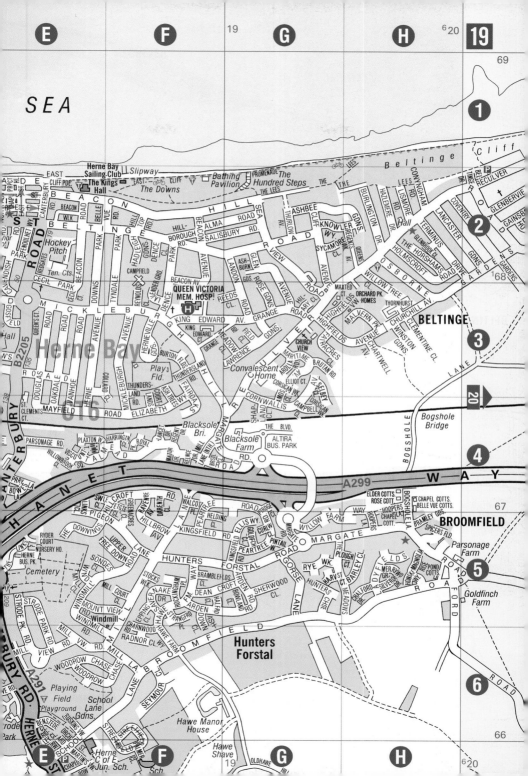

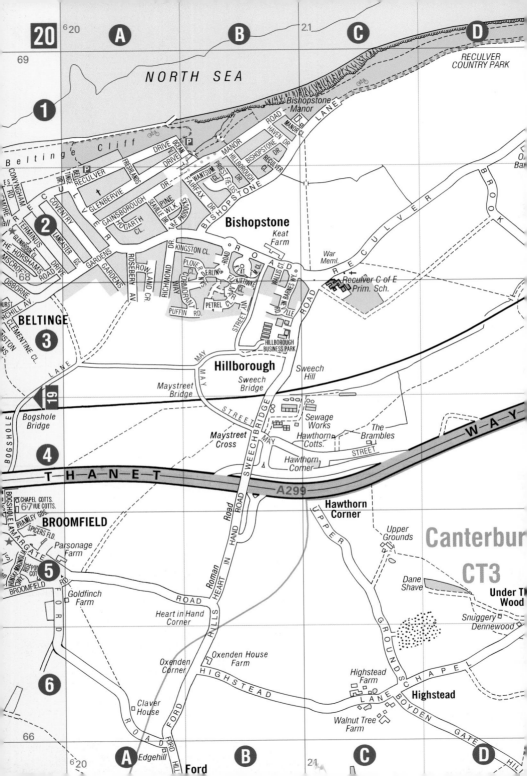

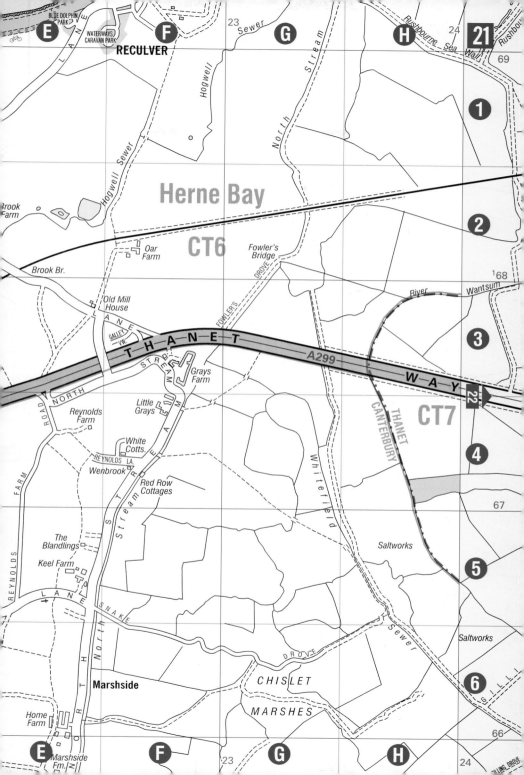

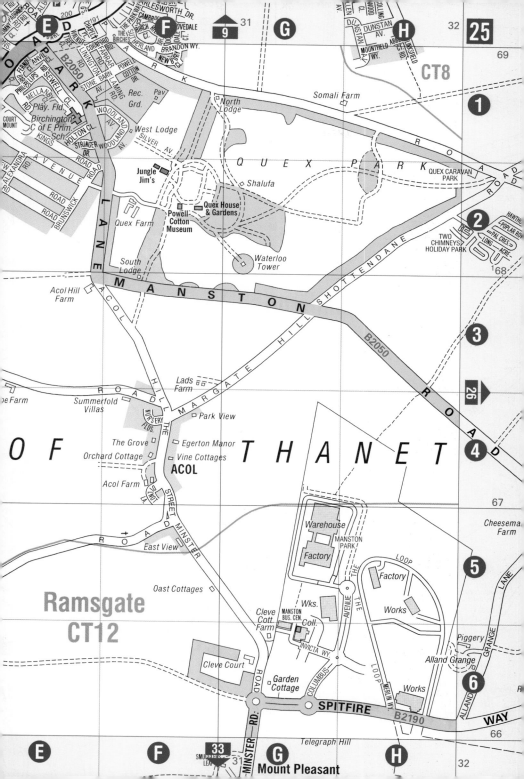

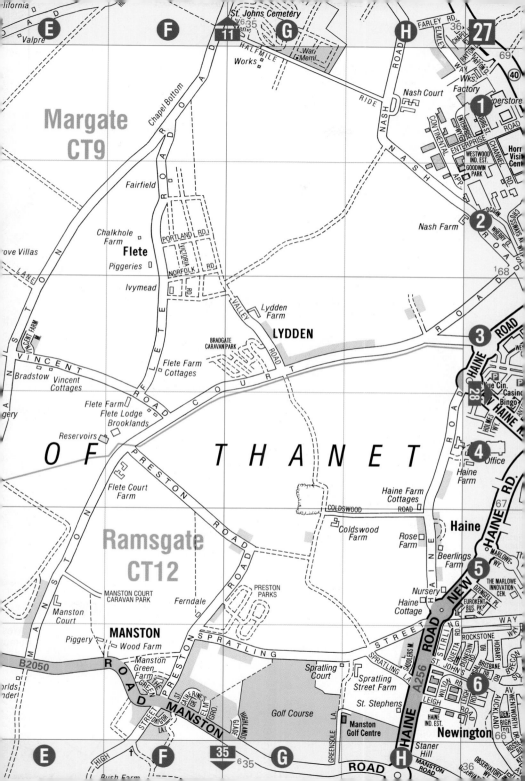

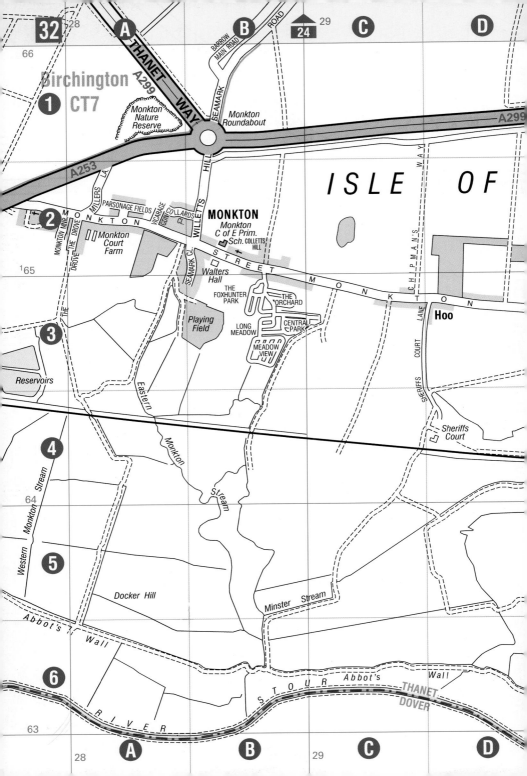

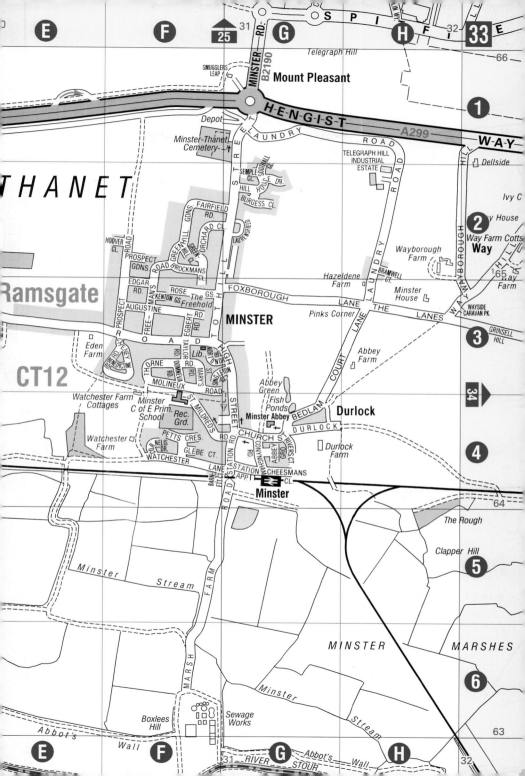

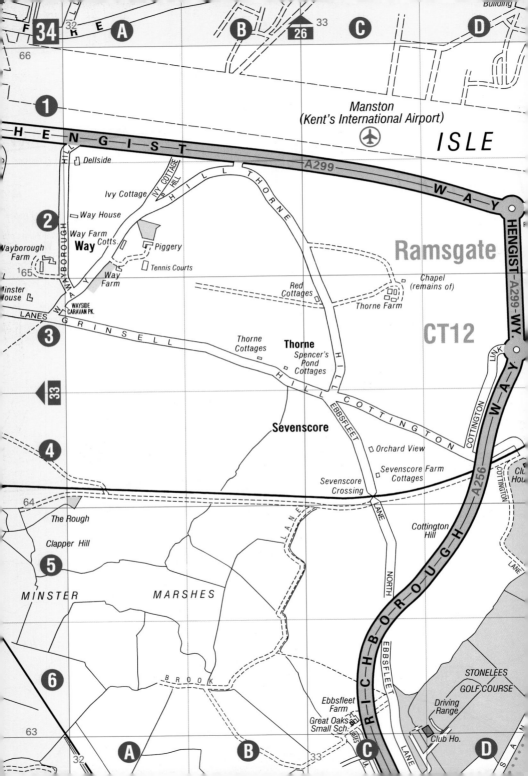

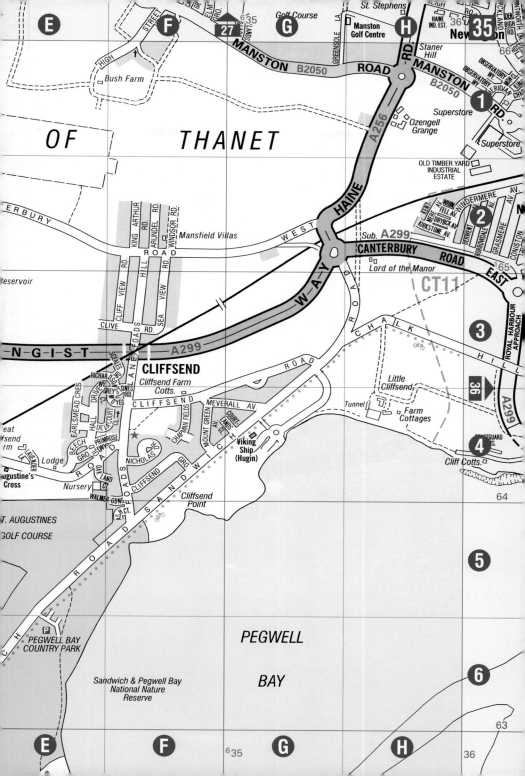

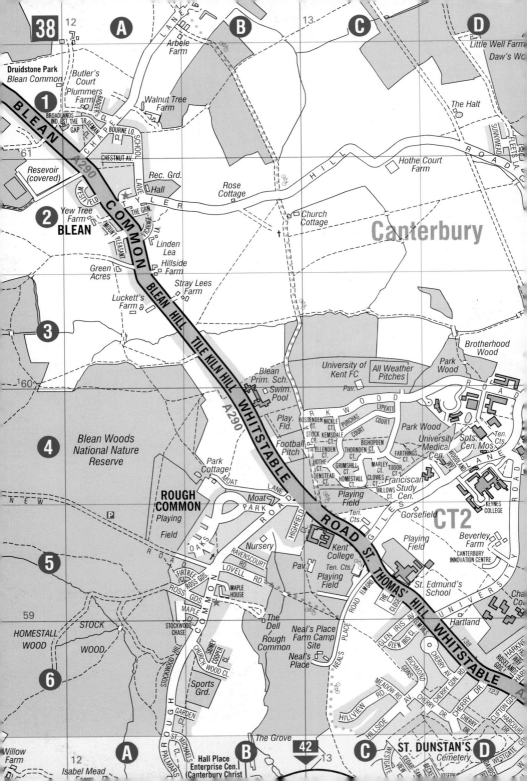

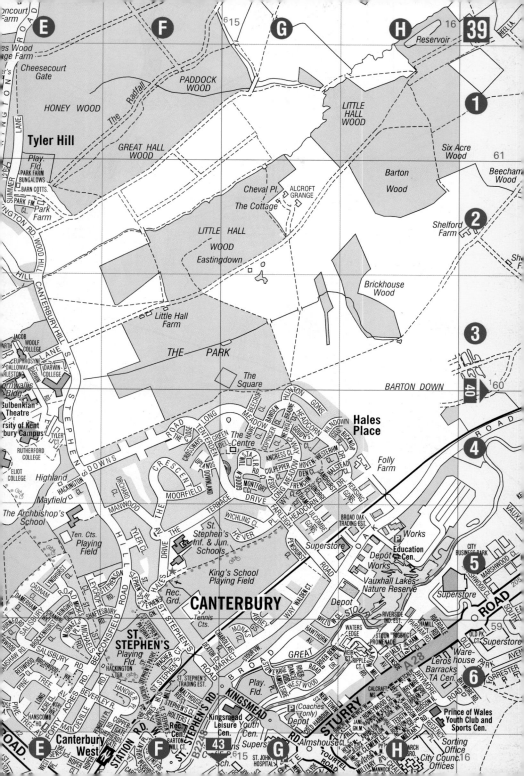

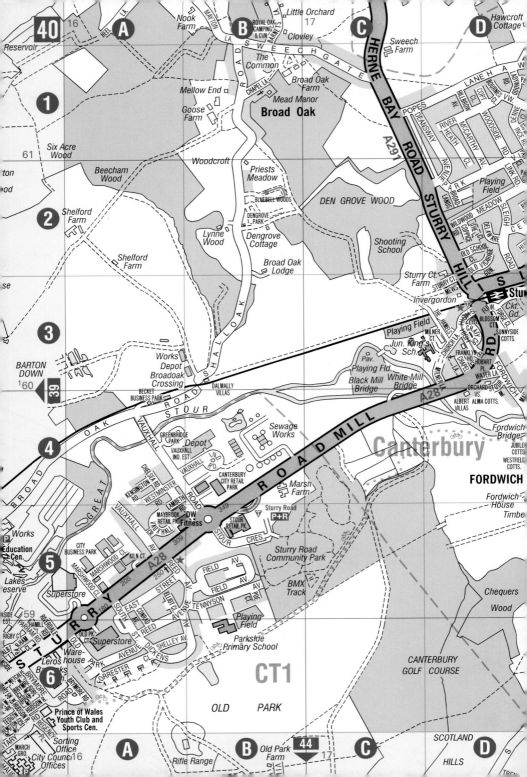

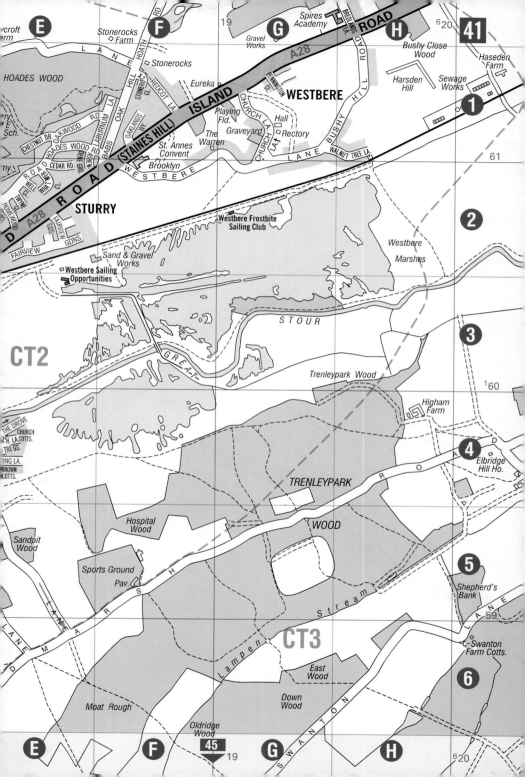

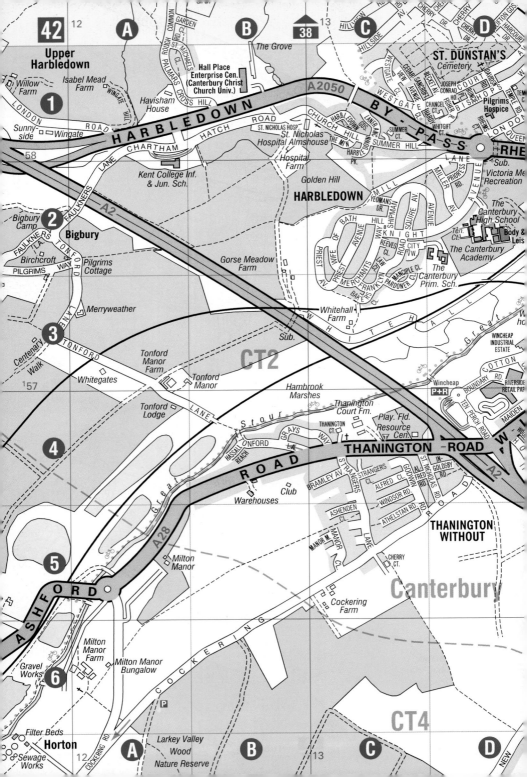

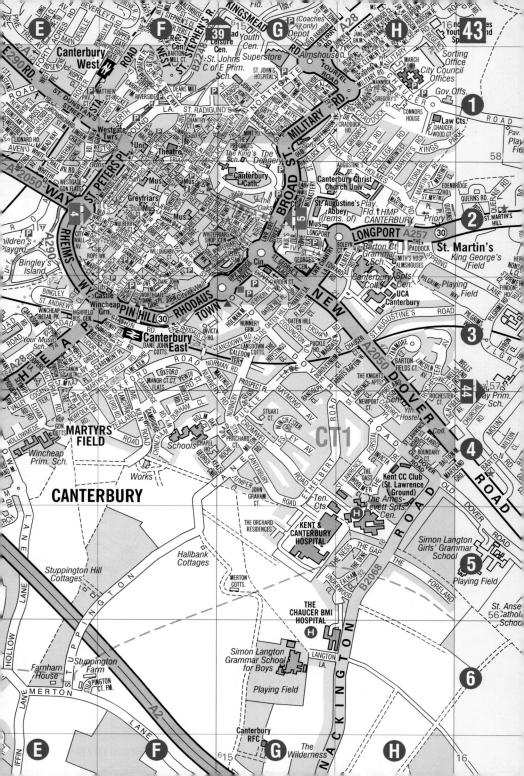

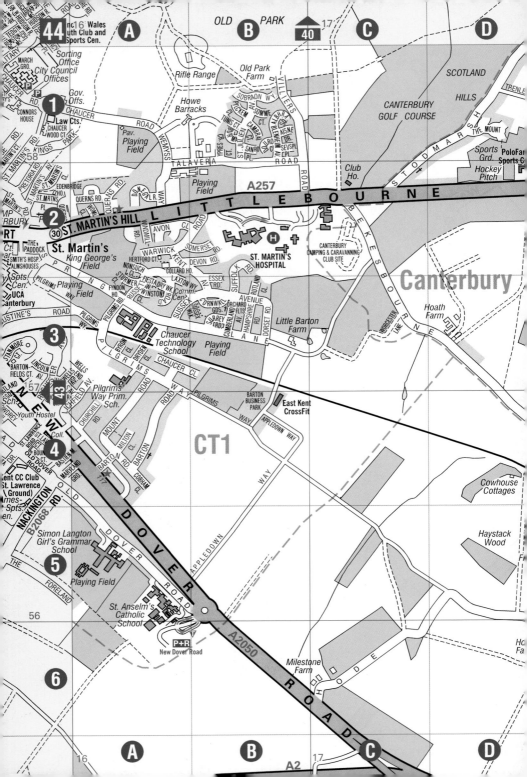

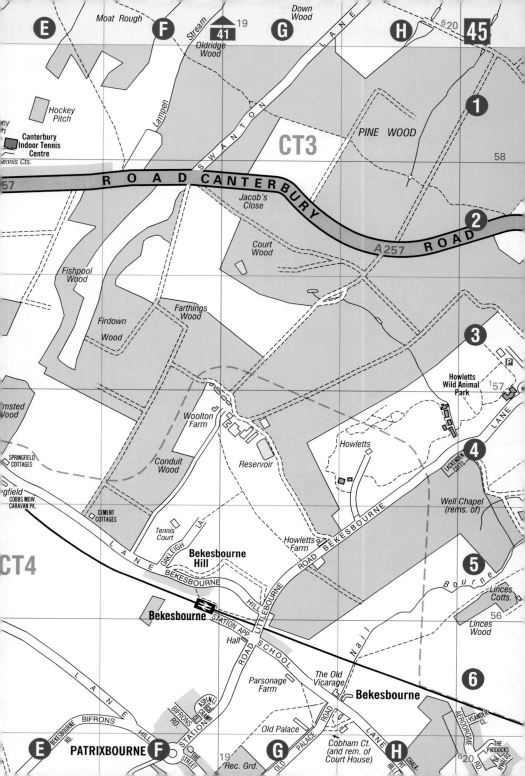

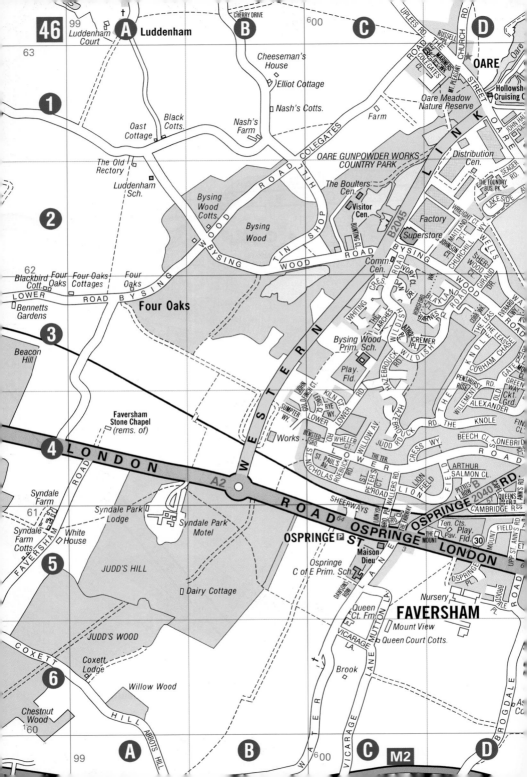

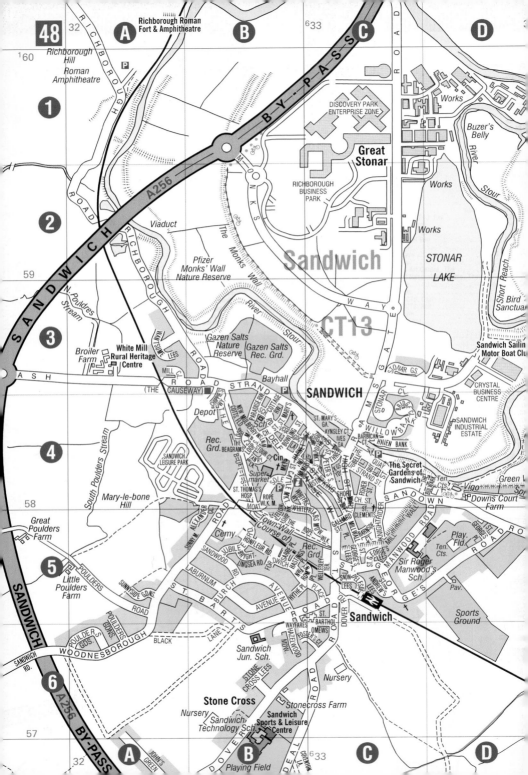

INDEX

Including Streets, Places & Areas, Hospitals etc., Industrial Estates,
Selected Flats & Walkways, Stations and Selected Places of Interest.

HOW TO USE THIS INDEX

1. Each street name is followed by its Postcode District, then by its Locality abbreviation(s) and then by its map reference;
e.g. **Abbey St.** ME13: Fav . . . . **3F 47** is in the ME13 Postcode District and the Faversham Locality and is to be found in square 3F on page **47**.
The page number is shown in bold type.

2. A strict alphabetical order is followed in which Av., Rd., St., etc. (though abbreviated) are read in full and as part of the street name;
e.g. **Crossley Av.** appears after **Cross La.** but before **Cross Rd.**

3. Streets and a selection of flats and walkways that cannot be shown on the mapping, appear in the index with the thoroughfare to which they are
connected shown in brackets; e.g. **Artillery Ho.** CT1: Cant . . . . 1G **43** (off Victoria Row)

4. Addresses that are in more than one part are referred to as not continuous.

5. Places and areas are shown in the index in **BLUE TYPE** and the map reference is to the actual map square in which the town centre or area
is located and not to the place name shown on the map; e.g. **BELTINGE** **2H 19**

6. An example of a selected place of interest is **Herne Bay Mus. & Gallery** **2D 18**

7. An example of a station is **Bekesbourne Station (Rail)** . . . . **5F 45**, also included is **Park & Ride**.
e.g. **New Dover Road (Park & Ride)** **6A 44**

8. An example of a Hospital, Hospice or selected Healthcare facility is **CHAUCER BMI HOSPITAL, THE** **6G 43**

9. Map references for entries that appear on large scale pages **4-7** are shown first, with small scale map references shown in brackets;
e.g. **Addington Pl.** CT11: Ram 5B **6** (3E **37**)

GENERAL ABBREVIATIONS

All. : Alley
App. : Approach
Arc. : Arcade
Av. : Avenue
Bri. : Bridge
Bungs. : Bungalows
Bus. : Business
Cen. : Centre
Circ. : Circle
Cir. : Circus
Cl. : Close
Coll. : College
Comn. : Common
Cnr. : Corner
Cott. : Cottage
Cotts. : Cottages
Ct. : Court
Cres. : Crescent
Cft. : Croft
Dr. : Drive
E. : East
Ent. : Enterprise
Est. : Estate

Fld. : Field
Flds. : Fields
Gdn. : Garden
Gdns. : Gardens
Ga. : Gate
Gt. : Great
Grn. : Green
Gro. : Grove
Hgts. : Heights
Ho. : House
Ho's. : Houses
Ind. : Industrial
Info. : Information
La. : Lane
Lit. : Little
Lwr. : Lower
Mnr. : Manor
Mans. : Mansions
Mkt. : Market
Mdw. : Meadow
Mdws. : Meadows
M. : Mews
Mt. : Mount

Mus. : Museum
Nth. : North
Pde. : Parade
Pk. : Park
Pas. : Passage
Pl. : Place
Prom. : Promenade
Ri. : Rise
Rd. : Road
Rdbt. : Roundabout
Shop. : Shopping
Sth. : South
Sq. : Square
St. : Street
Ter. : Terrace
Trad. : Trading
Up. : Upper
Vw. : View
Vs. : Villas
Vis. : Visitors
Wlk. : Walk
W. : West
Yd. : Yard

LOCALITY ABBREVIATIONS

Acol : **Acol**
Bek : **Bekesbourne**
Belt : **Beltinge**
Birch : **Birchington**
Blean : **Blean**
Brid : **Bridge**
B Oak : **Broad Oak**
B'stairs : **Broadstairs**
Bro E : **Brooks End**
Bkld : **Buckland**
Cant : **Canterbury**
Chart'm : **Chartham**
Ches : **Chestfield**
C'let : **Chislet**
C'snd : **Cliffsend**
Clift : **Cliftonville**
Darg : **Dargate**
Fav : **Faversham**

Ford : **Fordwich**
Garl : **Garlinge**
Good : **Goodnestone**
G'ney : **Graveney**
Harb : **Harbledown**
Hern : **Herne**
H Bay : **Herne Bay**
Hernh : **Hernhill**
Hoath : **Hoath**
L'brne : **Littlebourne**
Lud'm : **Luddenham**
Mans : **Manston**
Mgte : **Margate**
M'sde : **Marshside**
Minst : **Minster**
Monk'n : **Monkton**
Oare : **Oare**
Osp : **Ospringe**
Patr : **Patrixbourne**

Ram : **Ramsgate**
Rec : **Reculver**
R Comn : **Rough Common**
St N : **St Nicholas at Wade**
St Pet : **St Peter's**
S'wch : **Sandwich**
Seas : **Seasalter**
Sturry : **Sturry**
Swale : **Swalecliffe**
Tank : **Tankerton**
T Hill : **Tyler Hill**
Up Harb : **Upper Harbledown**
West : **Westbere**
Wgte S : **Westgate-on-Sea**
Whit : **Whitstable**
Wdchu : **Woodchurch**
Wdboro : **Woodnesborough**
Worth : **Worth**
York : **Yorkletts**

---

st Bowl
  Whitstable 2G **15**

A

bbey Ct. CT8: Wgte S 6H **9**
bbey Flds. ME13: Fav 4G **47**
bbey Flds. Ct. ME13: Fav 4G **47**
bbey Gdns. CT2: Cant 6G **39**

Abbey Ga. CT11: Ram 4B **36**
Abbey Gro. CT11: Ram 4B **36**
  CT12: Minst 4G **33**
Abbey Lodge CT11: Ram 5A **6**
Abbey Pl. ME13: Fav 3F **47**
Abbey Rd. ME13: Fav 3F **47**
Abbey School Sports Cen. 5E **46**
Abbey St. ME13: Fav 3F **47**
Abbots Barton Wlk. CT1: Cant 3H **43**
Abbots Hill CT11: Ram 4C **6** (3E **37**)
  ME13: Osp 6A **46**
Abbots Pl. CT1: Cant 1E **5** (1F **43**)
Abbots Rd. ME13: Fav 4G **47**

ACOL 4F **25**
Acol Hill CT7: Acol 3F **25**
Acton Rd. CT5: Whit 3F **15**
Ada Rd. CT1: Cant 4D **42**
Addington Pl. CT11: Ram 5B **6** (3E **37**)
Addington Rd. CT9: Mgte 3G **7** (3H **11**)
Addington Sq. CT9: Mgte 4G **7** (3H **11**)
Addington St. CT9: Mgte 4G **7** (3H **11**)
  CT11: Ram 5A **6** (3D **36**)
Addiscombe Gdns.
  CT9: Mgte 6H **7** (4H **11**)
Addiscombe Rd. CT9: Mgte 6H **7** (4A **12**)
Adelaide Gdns. CT11: Ram 5B **6** (3E **37**)

Adelaide Pl. CT1: Cant 4C 4 (2F 43)
Adeline CT2: Cant .3D 38
Adisham Way CT9: Mgte 4C 12
Admiralty Cl. ME13: Fav 3D 46
Admiralty Wlk. CT5: Whit 6C 14
Adrian Ct. CT8: Wgte S 4A 10
Adrian M. CT8: Wgte S 4B 10
Adrian Sq. CT8: Wgte S 4B 10
Aerodrome Rd. CT4: Bek 6H 45
Afghan Rd. CT10: St Pet 5F 13
Airedale Cl. CT9: Mgte 4A 12
Aisne Dr. CT1: Cant 1B 44
Albany Dr. CT6: H Bay 2B 18
Alberta Holiday Pk.
CT5: Seas 1A 30
Albert Ct. CT5: Whit 3F 15
CT11: Ram 4C 6
Albert M. CT9: Mgte 5G 7
CT11: Ram 5A 6
Albert Rd. CT1: Cant 2H 43
CT9: Mgte 3F 11
CT10: St Pet 5E 13
CT11: Ram 2F 37
Albert Row CT11: Ram 4C 36
Albert St. CT5: Whit 3F 15
CT11: Ram 5A 6 (3D 36)
Albert Ter. CT1: Cant 6H 39
CT9: Mgte 3E 7 (3G 11)
Albert Vs. CT2: Sturry 4D 40
Albion Ct. CT11: Ram 4C 6
Albion Hill CT11: Ram 4C 6 (3E 37)
Albion M. CT11: Ram 4D 6 (3E 37)
Albion Pl. CT1: Cant 1H 5 (1G 43)
CT9: Mgte 1G 7 (2H 11)
CT11: Ram 4C 6 (3E 37)
ME13: Fav 4E 47
Albion Rd. CT7: Birch 6E 9
CT9: Clift 2A 12
CT10: St Pet 1E 29
CT11: Ram 2D 6 (2F 37)
Albion St. CT10: B'stairs 3H 29
Albuhera Sq. CT1: Cant 1B 44
Alcroft Grange CT2: T Hill 2G 39
Alderney Gdns. CT10: St Pet 2E 29
Aldred Rd. ME13: Fav 5E 47
Aldridge Cl. CT6: H Bay 2H 17
Alexander Centre, The ME13: Fav 4F 47
Alexander Cl. CT13: S'wch 5B 48
ME13: Fav 3D 46
Alexander Dr. ME13: Fav 4D 46
Alexandra Ct. CT9: Mgte 3E 11
Alexandra Homes CT9: Mgte 6F 7 (4G 11)
Alexandra Rd. CT5: Whit 5E 15
CT7: Birch 2E 25
CT9: Mgte 6F 7 (5G 11)
CT10: B'stairs .3H 29
CT11: Ram 1A 6 (1D 36)
Alexandra Ter. CT9: Mgte 6F 7 (4G 11)
Alexandria Dr. CT6: H Bay 2A 18
Alfred Cl. CT1: Cant 4C 42
Alfred Cotts. CT11: Ram 2E 37
Alfred Rd. CT1: Cant 4C 42
CT7: Birch 5B 8
CT9: Mgte 4B 12
Alicia Av. CT9: Garl 5C 10
Alison Cl. CT7: Birch 5F 9
Alkali Row CT9: Mgte 2F 7
Alkham Cl. CT9: Clift 3F 13
Alland Grange La. CT12: Mans 6A 26
Allan Rd. CT5: Seas 6A 14
Allen Av. CT8: Wgte S 6H 9
Allenby Rd. CT12: Ram 4E 11
Alliance Rd. CT11: Ram 4D 6 (3F 37)
All Saints' Av. CT9: Mgte 4E 11
All Saints Cl. CT5: Whit 4G 15
All Saints Ct. CT1: Cant 2D 4
All Saints Ind. Est. CT9: Mgte 5E 7 (4G 11)
All Saints La. CT1: Cant 2D 4 (2F 43)
Alma Cotts. CT2: Sturry 4D 40
Alma Pl. CT1: Cant 1G 43
CT11: Ram 2C 6 (2E 37)
Alma Rd. CT6: H Bay 2F 19
CT9: Mgte 6G 7 (4H 11)
CT11: Ram 2B 6 (1E 37)
Alma St. CT1: Cant 1G 43
Almond Cl. CT5: Ches 4D 16
CT10: B'stairs .3C 28
Almshouses ME13: Fav 4E 47
Alpha Rd. CT7: Birch 6E 9
CT11: Ram 4A 6 (3D 36)
Altira Bus. Pk. CT6: H Bay 4G 19
Alvis Av. CT6: H Bay 2D 6
Amberley Ct. CT11: Ram 5G 47
Ambleside ME13: Fav 4B 46
Ambleside Pl. CT2: Cant 6G 39
Ames-Levett Sports Centre, The 4H 43

AMF Bowling
Margate 3G 7 (3H 11)
Amherst Cl. CT9: Mgte 4C 12
Amos Cl. CT6: Belt 4G 19
Anchor Hill CT9: Mgte 3H 7 (3G 11)
Ancress Cl. CT2: Cant 4G 39
Angel Ct. CT1: Cant 3F 5
Anna Pk. CT7: Birch 5D 8
Anne Cl. CT7: Birch 6F 9
Anne Grn. Wlk.
CT1: Cant 6H 39
Anne Ho. CT9: Mgte 2G 7
Anne's Rd. CT10: B'stairs 6H 13
Ann's Rd. CT11: Ram 1B 6 (1E 37)
Anson Cl. CT10: B'stairs 4D 28
Anthony Cl. CT12: Ram 1B 36
Anthony Cres. CT5: Whit 1D 30
Antolin Way CT12: Ram 4A 28
Anvil Cl. CT7: Birch 1E 25
Apple Craft Cen. .6G 47
Appledore Cl. CT9: Mgte 4C 12
Appledown Way CT1: Cant 4B 44
Applegarth Pk. CT5: Seas 1C 30
Approach Rd. CT9: Mgte 3A 12
CT10: B'stairs .3G 29
April Ri. CT5: Whit 6D 14
CT7: Birch 4C 8
Apsley Ct. CT11: Ram 3C 6
Arcadian, The CT9: Mgte 2F 7
(off Fort Hill)
Archway Ho. CT11: Ram 4B 6
Archway Rd. CT11: Ram 4B 6 (3E 37)
Arden Ct. CT1: Cant 6H 5 (3G 43)
Arden Rd. CT6: Broom 5F 19
ME13: Fav 4G 47
Arden Theatre
Faversham 4E 47
Argyle Av. CT9: Mgte 4E 11
Argyle Cen. CT11: Ram 4C 6
Argyle Gdns. CT9: Mgte 4E 11
Argyle Rd. CT5: Whit 4F 15
Argyll Dr. CT11: Ram 6E 29
Arkley Rd. CT6: H Bay 3D 18
Arklow Sq. CT11: Ram 2D 6 (2F 37)
Arlington Gdns. CT9: Mgte 5C 12
Arlington Ho. CT9: Mgte 3F 11
Arlington Sq. CT9: Mgte 3F 11
Armstrong Sq. CT6: H Bay 2G 11
Arnold Rd. CT9: Mgte 5G 7 (4H 11)
Arolla Rd. CT6: Belt 4G 19
Arran M. CT1: Cant 6H 39
Art for All (The Gallery)
Margate 3F 7 (3G 11)
Arthur Rd. CT7: Birch 5B 8
CT9: Mgte 2A 12
Arthur Salmon Cl. ME13: Fav 4D 46
Artillery Gdns. CT1: Cant 1G 43
Artillery Ho. CT1: Cant 1G 43
(off Victoria Row)
Artillery Rd. CT11: Ram 2D 6 (2F 37)
Artillery St. CT1: Cant 1G 43
Arundel Rd. CT9: Mgte 3B 12
CT12: C'snd 2F 35
Ascot Ct. CT9: Mgte 4G 7
Ascot Gdns. CT8: Wgte S 6A 10
Ashbee Gdns. CT6: Belt 2G 19
Ashburn Gdns. CT6: H Bay 2G 19
Ashburnham Rd. CT11: Ram 2B 36
Ash Cl. CT6: Hern .6D 18
CT10: B'stairs .3C 28
Ash Ct. CT12: C'snd 5F 35
Ashdown Cl. CT6: Broom 5F 19
Ashenden Cl. CT1: Cant 5C 42
Ashendene Gro. CT2: Sturry 1E 41
Ashford Cl. CT1: Cant, Chart'm 5A 42
CT4: Chart'm, Cant 5A 42
ME13: Fav 6E 47
Ashley Cl. CT12: Ram 5B 28
Ashley Dr. CT5: Seas 6C 14
Ash Rd. CT13: S'wch 3A 48
Ash Tree Cl. CT7: Birch 6F 9
(off The Parkway)
Ash Trees CT6: H Bay 3F 19
Ashurst Av. CT5: Whit 1E 31
Ashurst Gdns. CT9: Clift 2E 13
Aspinall Cl. CT4: Bek 6F 45
Astor Rd. CT10: B'stairs 5F 13
Athelstan Rd. CT1: Cant 5C 42
CT9: Mgte 2H 7 (2A 12)
ME13: Fav 5D 46
Athol Pl. ME13: Fav 3C 46
Athol Rd. CT5: Whit 3H 15
Auckland Av. CT12: Ram 6A 28
Audley Av. CT9: Mgte 4C 10
Augusta Pl. CT11: Ram 3D 6 (2F 37)

Augusta Rd. CT11: Ram 3D 6 (2F 37)
Augustine Rd. CT12: Minst 3F 33
Aurelie Way CT5: Whit 6H 15
Austin Av. CT6: H Bay 1F 17
Austins La. CT13: S'wch 4C 48
Avebury Av. CT11: Ram 1G 37
Avenue, The CT9: Mgte 5H 7 (4A 12)
Avenue Gdns. CT9: Clift 3C 12
Avenue Lodge CT11: Ram 2D 6
(off Avenue Rd.)
Avenue Rd. CT6: H Bay 2C 18
CT11: Ram 2D 6 (2F 37)
Avon Cl. CT1: Cant 2A 44
Avondale Cl. CT5: Whit 5A 16
Avondale Pl. CT5: Whit 3F 7
Aynsley Ct. CT13: S'wch 4C 48
Ayton Rd. CT11: Ram 3C 36

B

Babs Oak Hill CT2: Sturry 1F 41
Back La. CT1: Cant 4A 4 (2E 43)
ME13: Fav 4F 47
Backler Ho. CT9: Mgte 3A 12
(off Wilderness Hill)
Baddlesmere Rd. CT5: Tank 2A 16
Badgers Cl. CT2: Blean 1A 38
Baird's Hill CT10: B'stairs 1F 29
Bairdsley Cl. CT10: B'stairs 1F 29
(not continuous)
Bakers Cl. CT2: Cant 3C 42
Bakers Cl. CT11: Ram 3B 6
Bakery M. CT9: Mgte 6H 7
Balcomb Cres. CT9: Mgte 5C 12
Balcomb St. CT9: Mgte 5C 12
Baliol Rd. CT5: Whit 3G 15
Ballemoor Ct. CT11: Ram 6E 29
Balliol Rd. CT10: St Pet 5F 13
Balmoral Pl. CT11: Ram 3D 6 (3F 37)
Balmoral Rd. CT9: Garl 5D 10
Banks, The CT10: B'stairs 1F 29
Bank St. CT6: H Bay 2D 18
ME13: Fav 4E 47
Bannatyne's Health Club
Ramsgate 3B 28
Barbers Almshouses CT11: Ram 4A 6
(off Elms Av.)
Barbican Ct. CT13: S'wch 4C 48
Barges, The CT5: Whit 2G 15
Barley Cl. CT6: Broom 5H 19
Barn Cl. CT5: York 4C 30
Barn Cotts. CT2: T Hill 2E 39
Barn Cres. CT9: Mgte 4D 10
Barnes Av. CT9: Mgte 4D 10
Barnes Cl. ME13: Fav 3C 46
Barnes Ct. CT1: Cant 4D 4
(off St Jacob's Pl.)
Barnesende Ct. CT13: S'wch 5C 48
Barnes Way CT6: Belt 3B 20
Barnets La. CT8: B Oak 1B 44
Barnett Cl. CT12: Minst 4F 33
CT12: Ram 6B 28
Barnfield CT6: H Bay 5A 18
Barnfield ME13: Fav 3E 47
Barrington Cres. CT7: Birch 6F 9
Barrow Man Rd. CT7: Bro E, St N 4B 24
Barrows Cl. CT7: Birch 1E 25
Bartlett Dr. CT5: Whit 4A 16
Barton Bus. Pk. CT1: Cant 4B 44
Barton Ct. CT11: Ram 2C 6
Bartonfields Ct. CT1: Cant 3H 43
Barton Mill Ct. CT2: Cant 1F 43
Barton Mill Rd. CT1: Cant 6H 39
Barton Rd. CT1: Cant 4A 44
Bastien M. CT1: Cant 4H 43
Bath Pl. CT9: Mgte 3H 7 (2H 11)
Bath Rd. CT9: Mgte 3H 7 (3H 11)
Bathurst Ct. CT12: Ram 6B 28
Bawden Cl. CT2: Cant 4G 39
Bay M. CT6: H Bay .3E 19
Bay Sports Arena 4B 18
Bay Vw. CT6: H Bay 4B 18
(off Central Pde.)
Bay Vw. Hgts. CT7: Birch 5B 8
(off Ethelbert Rd.)
Bay Vw. Rd. CT10: B'stairs 5G 29
Bayview Rd. CT5: Whit 6F 15
Beach All. CT7: Whit 4C 8
(off Middle Wall)
Beach Av. CT7: Birch 5D 8
Beach Ct. Pk. CT5: Seas 6A 14
Beach Ho's. CT9: Mgte 3E 11
Beach Rd. CT8: Wgte S 4B 10
Beach Rd. CT8: Wgte S 4B 10
Beach St. CT6: H Bay 2D 18

Beach Wlk. CT5: Whit 2G **15**
Beacon Av. CT6: H Bay 2F **19**
Beacon Bingo
  Margate 4E **7**
Beacon Hgts. CT5: Tank 2H **15**
Beacon Hill CT6: H Bay 2E **19**
Beacon Rd. CT6: H Bay 2E **19**
  CT10: St Pet .1E **29**
Beaconsfield Gdns. CT10: St Pet 2F **29**
Beaconsfield Rd. CT2: Cant 6E **39**
Beaconsfields CT5: Seas 1B **30**
Beacon Wlk. CT6: H Bay 2E **19**
Beagrams, The CT13: S'wch 4B **48**
Beamont Cl. CT12: Mans 5B **26**
Beany, The
  House of Art & Knowledge 2E **5** (2F **43**)
Beatrice Rd. CT9: Mgte 5G **11**
Beaufort Av. CT12: Ram 1B **36**
Beaumanor CT6: H Bay 4E **19**
Beaumont Davy Cl. ME13: Fav 6E **47**
Beaumont Sq. CT6: H Bay 4A **18**
Beaumont Ter. ME13: Fav 5F **47**
Becket Av. CT2: Cant 1D **42**
Becket Bus. Pk. CT2: Cant 4A **40**
Becket Cl. CT5: Whit 4B **16**
Becket M. CT2: Cant 1F **43**
Beckett St. ME13: Fav 4E **47**
Bedford Ct. CT10: B'stairs 2H **29**
Bedford Sq. CT12: Ram 5B **28**
             (off Stirling Way)
Bedford Way CT7: St N 6F **23**
Bedlam Ct. La. CT12: Minst 4G **33**
Bedlington Sq. ME13: Fav 4F **47**
          (off Leslie Smith Dr.)
Beech Cl. ME13: Fav 4D **46**
Beechcroft CT5: Ches 4D **16**
Beechcroft Gdns. CT11: Ram 1F **37**
Beech Dr. CT10: B'stairs 3D **28**
Beech Gro. CT12: C'snd 4E **35**
Beecroft Cl. CT2: Cant 1G **43**
Beeping Bush Community Pharmacy Gallery
  . . . . .3F **7**
Beer Cart La. CT1: Cant 4C **4** (2F **43**)
BEKESBOURNE .6H **45**
BEKESBOURNE HILL 5F **45**
Bekesbourne Hill CT4: Bek 5F **45**
Bekesbourne La. CT3: Cant 2C **44**
  CT3: L'brne 5H **45**
  CT4: Bek 5H **45**
           (Lackenden Cotts.)
  CT4: Bek 2C **44**
           (Worcester La.)
Bekesbourne Rd. CT4: Brid 6E **45**
Bekesbourne Station (Rail) 5F **45**
Belgrave Cl. CT11: Ram 2A **6** (2D **36**)
Belgrave Rd. CT9: Mgte 4E **7** (3G **11**)
Bell CT2: Cant 3E **39**
Bell-Davies Dr. CT12: Mans 6B **26**
Bellevue Av. CT11: Ram 3D **6** (2F **37**)
Belle Vue Cotts. CT6: Broom 4H **19**
Belle Vue Rd. CT6: H Bay 2E **19**
Bellevue Rd. CT5: Whit 5H **15**
  CT11: Ram 3D **6** (2F **37**)
Bellflower M. CT1: Cant 4H **43**
          (off New Dover Rd.)
Bell La. CT13: S'wch 4C **48**
Belmont Cl. CT11: Ram 2A **6**
Belmont Ho. CT11: Ram 4C **36**
Belmont Rd. CT5: Whit 4F **15**
  CT8: Wgte S .5B **10**
  CT10: B'stairs 3G **29**
  CT11: Ram 2A **6** (2D **36**)
  ME13: Fav 5E **47**
Belmont St. CT11: Ram 2C **6** (2E **37**)
Belmont Yd. CT5: Whit 4F **15**
Belon Dr. CT5: Whit 6H **15**
BELTINGE 2H **19**
Beltinge Rd. CT6: Belt 2A **20**
Beltinge Rd. CT6: Belt, H Bay 2E **19**
Belton Cl. CT5: Whit 5G **15**
Belvedere Cl. ME13: Fav 3F **47**
Belvedere Rd. CT10: B'stairs 3H **29**
  ME13: Fav 3F **47**
Benacre Rd. CT5: Whit 1F **31**
Benedictine Rd. CT12: Minst 3F **33**
Bengal Rd. CT12: Ram 6A **28**
Bennells Av. CT5: Tank 3A **16**
Benstede Cl. CT6: Hern 6E **19**
Benstead Gro. ME13: Fav 4C **46**
Bentley Av. CT6: H Bay 1H **17**
Beresford Gap CT7: Birch 5D **8**
Beresford Gdns. CT9: Clift 2C **12**
Beresford Rd. CT5: Whit 4F **15**
  CT11: Ram 4A **6** (3D **36**)
Berkeley Rd. CT7: Birch 5D **8**
Best La. CT1: Cant 2D **4** (2F **43**)

Beverley Cl. CT7: Birch 5F **9**
Beverley Ho. CT2: Cant 6F **39**
         (off St Stephen's Rd.)
Beverley Rd. CT2: Cant 6E **39**
Beverley Way CT12: Ram 6C **28**
Bexley St. CT5: Whit 3F **15**
Bhutan Rd. CT6: Belt 3G **19**
Bicknor Cl. CT2: Cant 4H **39**
Biddenden Cl. CT9: Mgte 4C **12**
         (off Tenterden Way)
Bierce Ct. CT7: Birch 6D **8**
Bifrons Hill CT4: Patr 6E **45**
Bifrons Rd. CT4: Bek 6F **45**
BIGBURY 2A **42**
Bigbury Camp 2A **42**
Bigglestons Link CT1: Cant 5G **5**
Biggleswade Pas. CT1: Cant 3E **43**
Bilton Sq. CT9: Mgte 3F **7** (3G **11**)
Bingley St. CT1: Cant 6A **4** (3E **43**)
Binnie Cl. CT10: B'stairs 5F **29**
Birch Cl. CT10: B'stairs 4C **28**
Birches, The CT7: Birch 6F **9**
Birch La. CT7: Birch 6F **9**
BIRCHINGTON 6E **9**
Birchington-on-Sea Station (Rail) 6D **8**
Birch Rd. CT1: Cant 5E **43**
  CT5: Whit 5A **16**
Birchwood Wlk. CT2: Cant 6E **39**
Birds Av. CT9: Garl 6D **10**
Birkdale Gdns. CT6: H Bay 5B **18**
Birkdale Cl. CT5: Ches 5D **16**
Bishopden Ct. CT2: Cant 4C **38**
Bishop's Av. CT10: B'stairs 1H **29**
Bishops Courtyard CT1: Cant 5H **5**
BISHOPSTONE .2B **20**
Bishopstone Dr. CT6: Belt 1B **20**
Bishopstone La. CT6: Belt 2B **20**
Bishops Way CT2: Cant 1D **42**
Blackberry Way CT5: Whit 5B **16**
Blackburn Rd. CT6: H Bay 3H **17**
Blackfriars Cleary Gallery, The 1D **4**
Blackfriars St. CT1: Cant 1E **5** (1F **43**)
Black Griffin La. CT1: Cant 3B **4** (2F **43**)
Black La. CT13: S'wch 6A **48**
Blackstable Ct. CT5: Whit 5F **15**
Blake Ct. CT11: Ram 1D **36**
Blaxland Cl. ME13: Fav 3D **46**
BLEAN 2A **38**
Blean Comn. CT2: Blean 1A **38**
Blean Hill CT2: Blean 3A **38**
Blean Vw. Rd. CT6: H Bay 3H **17**
Blean Woods National Nature Reserve 4A **38**
  ME13: Fav 6G **47**
Blenheim Av. CT1: Cant 1B **44**
Blenheim Cl. CT6: Hern 6E **19**
  CT10: B'stairs 4D **28**
Bloomsbury Rd. CT11: Ram 3C **36**
Blossom Ct. CT2: Sturry 3D **40**
Bluebell Woods CT7: B Oak 2B **40**
Blueberry Cl. CT10: B'stairs 5F **29**
Blue Dolphin Pk. CT6: Rec 1E **21**
Bluefield M. CT5: Whit 1E **31**
          (off Old Farm Cl.)
Body & Mind Leisure
  Canterbury 2D **42**
Bognor Dr. CT6: H Bay 3B **18**
Bogshole La. CT5: Whit 3F **31**
  CT6: Broom, H Bay 4H **19**
          (not continuous)
Boleyn Av. CT9: Mgte 4C **10**
Boleyn Ct. CT1: Cant 2H **43**
Bolton St. CT11: Ram 1D **36**
Bonners All. CT5: Whit 3F **15**
            (off High St.)
Boorman Way CT5: Whit 5G **15**
Booth Pl. CT9: Mgte 2H **7** (2H **11**)
Borough, The CT1: Cant 1F **5** (1G **43**)
Borrowdale Av. CT11: Ram 2A **36**
Borstal Av. CT5: Whit 1F **31**
Borstal Hill CT5: Whit 1F **31**
Bossenden Ct. CT2: Cant 4C **38**
Botany Rd. CT7: Birch 4E **13**
Boughton Av. CT10: B'stairs 5G **29**
Boulevard, The CT6: H Bay 5A **18**
  CT8: Wgte S .5A **10**
Boundary Chase CT5: Whit 5B **16**
Boundary Rd. CT1: Cant 4H **43**
  CT11: Ram 2B **6** (2E **37**)
Bourne Lodge Cl. CT2: Blean 1A **38**
Bournemouth Dr. CT6: H Bay 2B **18**
Bournes Cl. CT2: Sturry 1D **40**
Bowen Ct. CT11: Ram 2D **36**
Bowes Av. CT9: Mgte 4C **10**
Bowes Ct. CT5: Tank 3A **16**

Bowes La. CT6: H Bay 4E **19**
Bowland Ct. CT6: Broom 5G **19**
Bowling St. CT13: S'wch 4B **48**
Bowyer Rd. CT5: Seas 6B **14**
Boyden Ga. Hill CT3: C'let 6C **20**
Brabourne Cl. CT2: Cant 4G **39**
Bracken Ct. CT10: St Pet 2E **29**
Bradgate Caravan Pk. CT9: Mgte 3F **27**
Bradley Rd. CT12: Ram 6C **28**
Bradstow Way CT10: B'stairs 2F **29**
Bramblefields Cl. CT6: Broom 5F **19**
Bramblehill Rd. ME13: Fav 3E **47**
Bramble La. CT9: Mgte 2D **26**
Bramcote Wlk. CT11: Ram 2C **36**
Bramley Av. CT1: Cant 4C **42**
  ME13: Fav 5G **47**
Bramley Gdns. CT6: Broom 5H **19**
Bramshaw Rd. CT2: Cant 6E **39**
Bramwell Ct. CT12: Minst 2H **33**
Brandon Rd. CT12: Ram 6A **28**
Brandon Way CT7: Birch 1F **25**
Brassey Av. CT10: B'stairs 4F **29**
Brecon Sq. CT12: Ram 6A **28**
Bredlands La. CT2: West 1H **41**
Brent Hill ME13: Fav 3E **47**
Brent Rd. ME13: Fav 3E **47**
BRENTS, THE 3F **47**
Brents Ind. Est. ME13: Fav 2F **47**
Brewhouse, The ME13: Fav 3F **47**
           (off Court St.)
Brian Roberts Ho. CT6: H Bay 2D **18**
Briars, The CT5: Whit 1E **31**
Briars Wlk. CT10: B'stairs 4F **29**
Briary Cl. CT9: Garl 5B **10**
Bridewell Pk. CT5: Whit 4A **16**
Bridge Approach, The CT5: Whit 4H **15**
Bridge Cl. CT13: S'wch 4C **48**
Bridge Country & Leisure Pk. CT5: Seas . . .1A **30**
Bridgefield Ct. CT5: Tank 2B **16**
Bridgefield Rd. CT5: Swale, Tank 2B **16**
Bridge Ho. CT11: Ram 2C **36**
Bridge Rd. CT9: Mgte 5C **10**
  ME13: Fav 3E **47**
Bridges Cl. CT7: St N 5E **23**
Bridgeway CT5: Whit 4H **15**
Bridle Way CT6: H Bay 4B **18**
Bridleway Gdns. CT10: B'stairs 4E **29**
Briganda Wlk. CT11: Ram 1C **6**
Bright Ho. CT11: Ram 2D **6**
Brightlingsea Rd. CT13: S'wch 5B **48**
Bright's Pl. CT11: Ram 2D **6** (2E **37**)
Brindle Gro. CT11: Ram 6F **29**
Brisbane Dr. CT12: Ram 6A **28**
Bristol Cl. CT6: H Bay 4F **19**
Bristol Pl. CT11: Ram 2A **6** (2D **36**)
Bristol Rd. CT11: Cant 4F **43**
Britannia Av. CT5: Whit 6D **14**
Briton Rd. ME13: Fav 4E **47**
Broadgate Hall CT11: Ram 2F **37**
          (off Thanet Rd.)
Broadlands CT2: Sturry 2D **40**
Broadlands Ind. Est. CT2: Blean 1A **38**
Broadley Av. CT7: Birch 2D **24**
Broadley Rd. CT9: Mgte 6C **12**
  CT10: St Pet .6C **12**
BROAD OAK 1B **40**
Broad Oak Rd. CT2: Cant 6G **39**
Broad Oak Trad. Est. CT2: Cant 5H **39**
BROADSTAIRS 3H **29**
Broadstairs Retail Pk. CT10: B'stairs 3B **28**
Broadstairs Rd. CT10: St Pet 2D **28**
Broadstairs Sailing Club 3H **29**
Broadstairs Station (Rail) 2G **29**
Broad St. CT1: Cant 1G **5** (1G **43**)
  CT9: Mgte 2F **7** (2G **11**)
  CT11: Ram 3B **6** (2E **37**)
Broadway, The CT6: H Bay 2A **18**
  CT10: B'stairs, St Pet 3G **29**
  CT11: Ram 3D **36**
Brockenhurst Cl. CT2: Cant 6E **39**
Brockenhurst Rd. CT11: Ram 1F **37**
Brockley Rd. CT9: Mgte 3H **7** (3H **11**)
Brockmans Cl. CT12: Minst 2F **33**
Brogdale Pl. ME13: Osp 5D **46**
Brogdale Rd. ME13: Osp 6D **46**
BROMSTONE 4E **29**
Bromstone M. CT10: B'stairs 4E **29**
Bromstone Rd. CT10: B'stairs 4E **29**
Brook Cl. CT6: H Bay 4A **18**
Brooke Av. CT9: Garl 6D **10**
Brooklands Cl. CT2: Ford 4D **40**
  CT6: H Bay 1G **17**
Brook La. CT6: H Bay, Rec 2D **20**
  CT12: Ram 6A **34**
Brook Rd. CT5: Swale 2C **16**
  ME13: Fav 3E **47**

BROOKS END .3C 24
BROOMFIELD 5H 19
Broomfield Cres. CT9: Clift 3F 13
Broomfield Rd. CT6: Broom, Hern 6F 19
   ME13: Fav 2E 47
Brown Cotts. CT2: Ford 4E 41
Brunswick Ct. CT11: Ram 2C 6
Brunswick Rd. CT7: Birch 2E 25
Brunswick Sq. CT6: H Bay 2C 18
Brunswick St. CT11: Ram 3C 6 (2E 37)
Brymore Cl. CT1: Cant 6H 39
Brymore Rd. CT1: Cant 6H 39
Buckhurst Dr. CT9: Clift 3F 13
Buckingham Rd. CT5: Swale 3B 16
   CT9: Mgte 6F 7 (4G 11)
   CT10: B'stairs 3H 29
Buenos Ayres CT9: Mgte 3F 11
Bugsy's Ten Pin Bowling 2A 12
Buller Gro. CT5: Seas 1D 30
Buller's Av. CT6: H Bay 3B 18
BULLOCKSTONE 6B 18
Bullockstone Rd. CT6: H Bay 5B 18
Bulwark, The CT13: S'wch 4D 48
Bunting Cl. ME13: Fav 2C 46
Burch Av. CT13: S'wch 5B 48
Burgate CT1: Cant 3F 5 (2G 43)
Burgate La. CT1: Cant 4G 5 (2G 43)
Burgess Cl. CT12: Minst 2G 33
Burlington Dr. CT6: Belt 2H 19
Burlington Gdns. CT9: Mgte 5E 11
Burma Cres. CT1: Cant 1B 44
Burnan Rd. CT5: Swale 3C 16
Bursill Cres. CT12: Ram 6B 28
Burton Flds. CT6: H Bay 4H 19
Bush Av. CT12: Ram 6B 28
Bushy Hill Rd. CT2: West 1G 41
Butchery, The CT13: S'wch 4C 48
Butchery La. CT1: Cant 3E 5 (2F 43)
Buttermere ME13: Fav 5G 47
Butts, The CT13: S'wch 4B 48
Buxton Ct. CT12: Ram 5B 28
Byron Av. CT9: Mgte 5H 7 (4H 11)
Byron Cl. CT1: Cant 3A 44
Bysing Wood Rd. ME13: Fav, Lud'm 3A 46

C

Cadnam Cl. CT2: Cant 5E 39
Caernarvon Gdns. CT10: B'stairs 2H 29
Cages Cl. CT5: Whit 5E 15
Calais Hill CT2: T Hill 2D 38
Calcraft M. CT1: Cant 6H 39
Caledon Ter. CT1: Cant 3G 43
Callis Ct. Rd. CT10: B'stairs 1F 29
Calverden Rd. CT12: Ram 6A 28
Cambourne Av. CT8: Wgte S 5H 9
Cambrai Ct. CT1: Cant 1B 44
Cambrian Cotts. CT11: Ram 3D 36
Cambridge Ct. CT7: Birch 6F 9
Cambridge Rd. CT1: Cant 3F 43
   ME13: Fav 5D 46
Cambridge Ter. CT9: Mgte 4B 12
Cambridge Way CT1: Cant 4F 43
Camden Cotts. CT11: Ram 3C 6
Camden Rd. CT10: St Pet 6E 13
   CT11: Ram 4C 6 (3E 37)
Camden Sq. CT11: Ram 3C 6 (2E 37)
Camellia Cl. CT9: Mgte 5D 10
Campbell Cl. CT6: Belt 4G 19
Campfield CT6: H Bay 2F 19
Cannogate Ct. CT11: Ram 5A 6
Cannonbury Rd. CT11: Ram 5A 6 (3D 36)
Cannon M. CT11: Ram 2A 6
Cannon Rd. CT11: Ram 3A 6 (2D 36)
Canon Appleton Ct. CT1: Cant 3E 43
CANTERBURY 3E 5 (2F 43)
Canterbury Camping & Caravanning Club Site
   CT3: Cant 2C 44
Canterbury Castle 6B 4 (3F 43)
Canterbury Cathedral 2F 5 (2G 43)
Canterbury Christ Church University
   Northwood Rd. 3C 28
   Nth. Holmes Rd. 2H 5 (2G 43)
   Up. Chantry La. 6H 5
Canterbury City Retail Pk. CT1: Cant 4B 40
Canterbury Ct. CT10: St Pet 2D 28
Canterbury East Station (Rail) 3F 43
Canterbury Environmental Education Cen. .5H 39
Canterbury Environment Centre 1E 5
Canterbury Golf Course 2C 44
Canterbury Heritage Mus. 3C 4 (2F 43)
Canterbury Hill CT2: T Hill 3E 39
Canterbury Historic River Tours 2D 4
Canterbury Indoor Tennis Cen. 1E 45
Canterbury Innovation Cen. CT2: Cant 5D 38
Canterbury La. CT1: Cant 4F 5 (2G 43)
Canterbury Punting Company, The 3C 4
Canterbury RFC 6G 43
Canterbury Rd. CT3: L'brne 2G 45
   CT5: Whit 5F 15
   CT6: H Bay 4E 19
   CT6: Hern 5E 19
   CT7: Birch, Bro E, St N 6F 23
   CT8: Birch, Wgte S 4H 23
   CT9: Mgte 5C 10
   ME13: Fav 5F 47
Canterbury Rd. E. CT11: Ram 3A 36
   CT12: Ram .2H 35
Canterbury Rd. W. CT12: C'snd 2E 35
Canterbury Roman Mus. 3F 5
Canterbury Tales, The 3E 5 (2F 43)
Canterbury Vis. Cen. 2D 4
Canterbury West Station (Rail) 1F 43
Canute Rd. CT7: Birch 5B 8
   ME13: Fav 5E 47
Capel Cl. CT10: B'stairs 4F 13
Capel Rd. ME13: Fav 4D 46
Carausius Ct. CT1: Cant 4C 4
Carey Ho. CT1: Cant 3F 43
       (off Station Rd. E.)
Carlton Av. CT10: B'stairs 2G 29
   CT11: Ram 4A 6 (3D 36)
Carlton Cinema
   Westgate-on-Sea 4A 10
Carlton Ct. CT5: Whit 4H 15
Carlton Hill CT6: H Bay 3A 18
Carlton Mans. CT9: Clift 2A 12
Carlton Ri. CT8: Wgte S 5G 9
Carlton Rd. CT5: Whit 5F 31
Carlton Rd. E. CT8: Wgte S 5H 9
Carlton Rd. W. CT8: Wgte S 5G 9
Carmel Ct. CT7: Birch 5D 8
       (off Gainsborough Rd.)
Carn Brea CT9: Mgte 3H 7 (3H 11)
Carn Brea Cotts. CT9: Mgte 3H 7
Carnoustie Cl. CT5: Ches 5E 17
Caroline Cl. CT5: Whit 1D 30
Caroline Cotts. CT9: Mgte 2H 7
Caroline Cres. CT10: St Pet 1E 29
Caroline Sq. CT9: Mgte 2H 7 (2H 11)
Carriage M. CT2: Cant 1F 43
Carroway's Pl. CT9: Mgte 3G 7 (3H 11)
Caslocke St. ME13: Fav 4E 47
Castle Av. CT10: B'stairs 1H 29
Castle Mayne Av. CT7: Wdchu 4B 26
Castle Rd. CT5: Whit 3G 15
Castle Row CT1: Cant 6C 4 (3F 43)
Castle St. CT1: Cant 6B 4 (3F 43)
Catherine Way CT10: B'stairs 1G 29
Cattle Mkt. CT13: S'wch 4B 48
Causeway, The CT1: Cant 1F 43
   CT13: S'wch 3F 48
Cavendish Ct. CT6: H Bay 2E 19
       (off Cavendish Rd.)
Cavendish Pl. CT11: Ram 4B 6 (3E 37)
Cavendish Rd. CT6: H Bay 3E 19
Cavendish St. CT11: Ram 3B 6 (2E 37)
Cavour Rd. ME13: Fav 4E 47
Caxton Rd. CT9: Garl 5D 10
Cecil Ct. CT6: H Bay 3E 19
Cecilia Apartments CT11: Ram 1E 37
Cecilia Gro. CT10: St Pet 1F 29
Cecilia Rd. CT11: Ram 1D 6 (1E 37)
Cecil Pk. CT6: H Bay 2E 19
Cecil Sq. CT9: Mgte 3F 7 (3G 11)
Cecil St. CT9: Mgte 3F 7 (3G 11)
Cedar Cl. CT7: Birch 6F 9
       (off The Parkway)
   CT9: Mgte 4B 12
   CT10: St Pet 6F 13
Cedar Rd. CT2: Sturry 3F 33
Cedarview CT2: Cant 1C 42
Cedric Rd. CT8: Wgte S 4A 10
Cement Cotts. CT4: Bek 5F 45
Central Av. CT6: H Bay 2B 18
Central Pde. CT6: H Bay 2C 18
Central Pk. CT12: Monk'n 3B 32
Central Rd. CT11: Ram 1A 6 (1D 36)
Centre, The CT9: Mgte 3F 7 (3G 11)
   CT12: Ram .6A 28
Century Rd. ME13: Fav 4G 47
Chafy Cres. CT2: Sturry 3D 40
Chain, The CT13: S'wch 5C 48
Chalford Dr. CT6: Broom 5H 19
Chalk Hill CT11: Ram 3H 35
Chalkpit Hill CT4: Bek 6H 45
Challock Ct. CT9: Clift 3F 13
Chalkpit Hill CT4: Bek 6H 45
Chamberlain Dr. CT6: H Bay 1H 17
Chambers Wall CT7: St N 4B 22
Chambers Wharf ME13: Fav 2G 47
Chambers Wharf La. ME13: Fav 3G 47
Chancel Ct. CT2: Cant 1D 42
Chanctonbury Chase CT5: Seas 1C 30
Chandos Rd. CT10: B'stairs 3H 29
Chandos Sq. CT10: B'stairs 3H 29
Chandos Ter. CT11: Ram 2B 6
Channel Rd. CT9: Mgte 1A 28
Channel Vw. Ct. CT11: Ram 2F 37
       (off Granville Marina)
Chantry Cl. CT1: Cant 1F 43
Chantry Hall CT1: Cant 6D 4
Chapel Cott. CT6: Broom 5H 19
Chapel Cotts. CT6: Broom 4H 19
Chapel Ct. CT9: Mgte 3G 7
Chapel Hill CT9: Mgte 6H 11
Chapel Hill Cl. CT9: Mgte 6H 11
Chapel Ho. CT1: Cant 4F 43
Chapel La. CT2: B Oak 1B 40
   CT2: Blean 1A 38
   CT2: Sturry .3D 40
   CT3: Hoath, M'sde 6D 20
Chapel Pl. CT7: Birch 6E 9
   CT11: Ram 3A 6 (2D 36)
Chapel Pl. La. CT11: Ram 3A 6 (2D 36)
Chapel Rd. CT11: Ram 2C 36
Chapel Row CT6: Hern 6E 19
Chapel St. CT6: H Bay 2E 19
   ME13: Fav 5F 47
Chapman Flds. CT12: C'snd 4F 35
Charing Cl. CT12: Ram 1C 36
Charing Cres. CT8: Wgte S 6H 9
Charles Drayson Ct. ME13: Fav 4G 47
       (off Gordon Sq.)
Charles Ct. CT11: Ram 1E 37
Charles St. CT6: H Bay 2D 18
Charleston Ct. CT2: Cant 3E 39
Charleston Ct. CT10: B'stairs 4H 29
       (off W. Cliff Rd.)
Charlesworth Dr. CT7: Birch 6F 9
Charlotte Ct. CT11: Ram 4C 6 (3E 37)
Charlotte M. CT1: Cant 3E 43
       (off Gordon Rd.)
Charlotte Pl. CT9: Mgte 5G 7 (4H 11)
Charlotte Sq. CT9: Mgte 4G 7 (3H 11)
Charlotte St. CT10: B'stairs 3H 29
Charlton Cl. CT1: Cant 5B 28
Charnwood CT5: Ches 4D 16
Charnwood Rd. CT6: Broom 6F 19
Charollais Cl. CT2: Cant 6G 39
Chart Cl. ME13: Fav 4D 46
Chart Gunpowder Mills 4D 46
Chartham Hatch Rd. CT2: Harb 1A 42
Chartham Ter. CT11: Ram 6A 6
Chartwell Av. CT6: Belt 3H 19
Chase, The CT5: Whit 5E 15
   CT11: Ram 6F 29
       (off Montefiore Av.)
Chatham Ct. CT11: Ram 1A 6 (1D 36)
Chatham Pas. CT11: Ram 2A 6
Chatham Pl. CT11: Ram 2B 6 (2E 37)
Chatham St. CT11: Ram 2A 6 (2D 36)
Chatsworth M. CT11: Ram 3C 36
Chaucer Av. CT5: Whit 4B 16
Chaucer BMI HOSPITAL, THE 6G 43
Chaucer Bus. Pk. CT5: Whit 1E 31
Chaucer Cl. CT1: Cant 3A 44
Chaucer Ct. CT1: Cant 3H 43
Chaucer Rd. CT1: Cant 1H 43
   CT10: B'stairs 4G 29
Chaucer Wood Ho. CT1: Cant 1H 43
Cheesmans Cl. CT12: Minst 4G 33
Chelsea Rd. CT1: Cant 4A 40
Cheney Rd. CT12: Minst 3F 33
   ME13: Fav 4H 47
Cheriton Av. CT12: Ram 1B 36
Cherry Av. CT2: Cant 6D 38
Cherry Ct. CT1: Cant 5C 42
Cherry Dr. CT2: Cant 6C 38
   ME13: Lud'm 1B 46
Cherry Gdn. Rd. CT2: Cant 6D 38
Cherry Gdns. CT6: H Bay 3C 18
   CT10: B'stairs 4C 28
Cherry Orchard CT5: Ches 5C 16
Cherry Tree Gdns. CT12: Ram 4B 28
Chester Rd. CT8: Wgte S 5B 10
CHESTFIELD 4C 16
Chestfield and Swalecliffe Station (Rail) . .3D 16
Chestfield Golf Course 5D 16
Chestfield Ind. Est. CT5: Ches 3B 16
Chestfield Rd. CT5: Ches 4C 16
Chestnut Av. CT2: Blean 1A 38
Chestnut Dr. CT2: Sturry 1E 41
   CT6: H Bay 5B 18
   CT10: B'stairs 3D 28
Cheviot Ct. CT10: B'stairs 2H 29
Chichester Rd. CT12: Ram 6B 28

Chichester Wlk. CT12: Ram 6B 28
(off Chichester Rd.)
Childgate Rd. CT5: York 4B 30
Chilham Av. CT8: Wgte S 6H 9
CHILTON 3A 36
Chilton La. CT11: Ram 3A 36
Chineham Way CT1: Cant 4F 43
Chipman's Way CT12: Minst 3C 32
Chippie's Way CT13: S'wch 4B 48
Chislet CT6: H Bay 2C 18
Christ Church Gate
Canterbury .3E 5
Chrysler Av. CT6: H Bay 1G 17
Church Av. CT11: Ram 3D 36
Church Cotts. CT2: Ford 4E 41
Church Ct. Gro. CT10: St Pet 1E 29
Churchfield Pl. CT9: Mgte 4F 7 (3G 11)
Churchfields CT9: Mgte 5G 7 (4H 11)
CT10: St Pet 6F 13
Church Hill CT2: Harb 1C 42
CT11: Ram 3B 6 (2E 37)
Churchill Av. CT6: Belt 3H 19
Churchill Ct. CT11: Ram 2D 36
(off High St.)
Churchill Rd. CT1: Cant 4A 44
Church Way ME13: Fav 2D 46
Church La. CT1: Cant 1G 43
(Knotts La.)
CT1: Cant 5B 4 (2F 43)
(Rosemary La.)
CT2: Ford .4E 41
CT2: Sturry 3D 40
CT2: West .1G 41
CT5: Seas .1C 30
Church Rd. CT9: Mgte 5H 7 (4H 11)
CT10: B'stairs 3H 29
CT11: Ram 3B 6 (2E 37)
ME13: Fav .4F 47
(East St.)
ME13: Fav .3F 47
(Upper Brents)
ME13: Oare 1D 46
Church Sq. CT10: B'stairs 3H 29
CHURCH STREET 4H 15
Church St. CT2: Cant 1E 43
CT5: Whit .4H 15
CT9: Mgte 5G 7 (4H 11)
CT10: St Pet 1E 29
CT12: Minst 4G 33
CT13: S'wch 4C 48
ME13: Fav .3F 47
Church St. St Mary's CT13: S'wch 4B 48
Church St. (St Paul's) CT1: Cant 4H 5
Church Vw. CT6: Belt 3G 19
Church Way CT5: Swale 2D 16
Church Wood Cl. CT2: R Comn 6B 38
Churchwood Dr. CT5: Ches 4D 16
Cinder Footpath CT10: B'stairs 3G 29
Circus, The CT6: H Bay 4C 18
City Bus. Pk. CT1: Cant 5A 40
City Vw. CT2: Cant 2C 42
City Wall Av. CT1: Cant 4A 4 (2E 43)
Claire Ct. CT10: B'stairs 2H 29
Clapham Cl. CT5: Whit 2E 31
Clare Dr. CT6: H Bay 3H 17
Claremont Gdns. CT11: Ram 2C 36
Claremont Pl. CT1: Cant 3F 43
CT11: Ram 1B 6 (1E 37)
Claremont St. CT6: H Bay 4A 18
Clarence Av. CT9: Clift 3D 12
Clarence Rd. CT6: H Bay 2B 18
CT11: Ram .3B 36
Clarence St. CT6: H Bay 2B 18
Clarendon Gdns. CT11: Ram 4A 6 (3D 36)
Clarendon M. CT10: B'stairs 3G 29
Clarendon Rd. CT9: Mgte 3A 12
CT10: B'stairs 3G 29
Clarendon St. CT6: H Bay 3A 18
Clare Rd. CT5: Whit 3G 7
Cleaver La. CT11: Ram 3C 6 (2E 37)
Clement Cl. CT1: Cant 1H 43
Clementine Cl. CT6: Belt 3H 19
Clement's Rd. CT12: Ram 5C 28
Cliff Av. CT6: Belt 2G 19
Cliff Dr. CT6: H Bay 3A 18
Cliffe Av. CT9: Mgte 4D 10
Cliff Fld. CT8: Wgte S 5G 9
Clifford Rd. CT5: Whit 5H 15
Cliff Prom. CT10: B'stairs 6H 13
Cliff Rd. CT5: Tank 2H 15
CT7: Birch .5C 8
CT10: B'stairs 6H 13
Cliff Sea Gro. CT6: H Bay 3A 18
LIFFSEND 4F 35
Cliffsend Gro. CT12: C'snd 4F 35

Cliffsend Rd. CT12: C'snd 4F 35
Cliffsend Rdbt. CT12: C'snd 2D 34
Cliffside Dr. CT10: B'stairs 6G 29
Cliff St. CT11: Ram 4B 6 (3E 37)
Cliff Ter. CT9: Mgte 1H 7 (2H 11)
Clifftown Gdns. CT6: H Bay 1H 17
Cliff Vw. CT12: C'snd 3F 35
Clifton Gdns. CT2: Cant 6D 38
CT9: Mgte 3H 7 (2H 11)
Clifton Lawn CT11: Ram 6A 6 (4D 36)
Clifton Pl. CT9: Mgte 2H 7 (2H 11)
Clifton Rd. CT5: Whit 5F 15
CT9: Mgte 3H 7 (3A 12)
CT11: Ram .1B 36
Clifton St. CT9: Mgte 2H 7 (2H 11)
CLIFTONVILLE .3C 12
Cliftonville Av. CT9: Mgte 3A 12
CT12: Ram .6B 28
Cliftonville Ct. CT9: Clift 2A 12
(off Edgar Rd.)
Cliftonville M. CT9: Clift 2A 12
Clive Rd. CT9: Mgte 2A 28
CT12: C'snd 3F 35
Cloisters, The CT1: Cant 1E 5
CT11: Ram 6A 6 (3D 36)
Close, The CT2: Cant 4F 39
(Crossways)
CT2: Cant .5C 38
(St Thomas' Hill)
ME13: Fav .5E 47
Clovelly Rd. CT5: Whit 6F 15
Clover Ri. CT5: Whit 4B 16
Clowes Ct. CT2: Cant 4C 38
Cluny Rd. ME13: Fav 4H 47
Clyde St. CT1: Cant 1G 43
Coach Ho. M. CT9: Clift 2B 12
Coastguard All. CT5: Whit 4E 15
Coastguard Cotts. CT6: H Bay 1F 17
CT11: Ram .4A 36
Coastguard Ho. Caravan Pk. CT6: H Bay 1F 17
Coastguards Cotts. CT11: Ram 2F 37
(off Victoria Pde.)
Cobb Ct. CT9: Mgte 2F 7
Cobblers Bri. Rd. CT6: H Bay 3B 18
Cobbs Mdw. Caravan Pk. CT4: Bek 4E 45
Cobbs Pl. CT9: Mgte 2F 7 (2H 11)
Cobb Wlk. ME13: Fav 3D 46
Cobden Pl. CT1: Cant 1F 5 (1G 43)
Cobham Chase ME13: Fav 3D 46
Cobham Cl. CT1: Cant 4A 44
Cockering Rd. CT1: Cant 6A 42
CT4: Cant, Chart'm 6A 42
Codrington Rd. CT11: Ram 3A 6 (2D 36)
Cogans Ter. CT1: Cant 4E 43
Coggan Ho. CT1: Cant 3F 43
(off Station Rd. E.)
Colburn Rd. CT10: B'stairs 5G 29
Cold Harbour CT1: Cant 6G 39
Coldswood Rd. CT12: Ram 4G 27
Colegates Cl. ME13: Oare 1C 46
Colegates Ct. ME13: Oare 1D 46
Colegates Rd. ME13: Oare 1C 46
Coleman Cres. CT12: Ram 5C 28
Coleman's Stairs CT7: Birch 5E 9
Coleman's Stairs Rd. CT7: Birch 5E 9
Coleman's Yd. CT11: Ram 4B 6 (3E 37)
Cole Rd. ME13: Fav 4G 47
Colette Cl. CT10: B'stairs 3G 13
Colette Ho. CT11: Ram 3B 6
Colewood Rd. CT5: Swale 2E 17
Collard Cl. CT6: H Bay 3F 19
Collard Ho. CT1: Cant 2A 44
Collards Cl. CT12: Monk'n 2A 32
College Gdns. CT8: Wgte S 5A 10
College Rd. CT1: Cant 2H 43
CT9: Mgte 6H 7 (5H 11)
CT11: Ram .1D 36
College Sq. CT8: Wgte S 6H 9
College Sq. Shop. Cen. CT9: Mgte 3F 7 (3H 11)
College Wlk. CT9: Mgte 3G 7
Colletts Hill CT12: Monk'n 2B 32
Collingwood Cl. CT8: Wgte S 6H 9
CT10: B'stairs 3E 29
Collingwood Ct. CT11: Ram 2A 6
Collingwood Rd. CT5: Whit 4E 15
Collins Rd. CT6: H Bay 5A 18
Colombo Sq. CT12: Ram 6A 28
Columbia Av. CT5: Whit 6D 14
Columbine Cl. CT5: Whit 1E 31
Columbus Ct. CT12: Mans 6G 25
Combined Court Cen.
Canterbury 1H 43
Conduit St. ME13: Fav 3F 47
Conference Wlk. CT1: Cant 2A 44
(off Russett Rd.)
Conifer Ct. CT8: Wgte S 4B 10

Coniston Av. CT11: Ram 2A 36
Connaught Bingo
Herne Bay .2D 18
Connaught Gdns. CT9: Mgte 6G 7 (4H 11)
Connaught Rd. CT9: Mgte 6G 7 (4H 11)
Connors Ho. CT1: Cant 1H 43
Conquest House
Canterbury 1E 5
Conrad Av. CT1: Cant 5A 40
Constable Rd. CT7: Birch 5E 9
Consul Cl. CT6: H Bay 1H 17
Continental App. CT9: Mgte 1H 27
Convent Rd. CT10: B'stairs 5F 13
Convent Wlk. CT11: Ram 4B 36
Conway Cl. CT7: Birch 6C 8
Conyngham Cl. CT12: Ram 5B 28
Conyngham Rd. CT6: Belt 2H 19
CT12: Minst 4G 33
Coombe Rd. CT9: Mgte 5C 30
Cooper Almshouses CT1: Cant 2H 43
(off Lwr. Chantry La.)
Coopers Hill CT6: H Bay 2D 18
Coopers La. CT1: Cant 3E 43
Copinger Cl. CT2: Cant 4G 39
Copperas Ct. CT5: Tank 2A 16
Copperfield Ct. CT1: Cant 6H 5
CT10: B'stairs 2H 29
Coppergate CT2: Cant 6F 39
Copperhurst Wlk. CT9: Clift 3E 13
Coppice, The CT2: Sturry 2D 40
Coppock Cl. CT12: Ram 6B 28
Copt Cl. CT2: Sturry 1D 40
Cordingham Cl. CT5: Seas 1C 30
Cormorant Way CT6: Belt 2B 20
Cornelis Dr. CT12: Minst 4F 33
Conford Rd. CT7: Birch 1E 25
Cornhill CT11: Ram 5B 6 (3E 37)
Cornminster Ct. CT6: H Bay 3B 18
Cornwall Av. CT11: Ram 1F 37
Cornwall Gdns. CT1: Cant 3B 44
CT9: Clift 3B 12
Cornwallis Av. CT6: Belt 4G 19
Cornwallis Circ. CT5: Whit 4E 15
Cornwallis Gdns. CT10: B'stairs 1G 29
Cornwall Rd. CT6: H Bay 3H 17
Coronation Cl. CT10: St Pet 6E 13
Coronation Cres. CT7: Garl 5D 10
Coronation Rd. CT5: Whit 2E 31
CT11: Ram .3D 36
Corsican Wlk. CT6: Belt 3G 19
(not continuous)
Corylus Dr. CT5: Whit 6C 14
Cossington Rd. CT1: Cant 3G 43
Cottage Rd. CT11: Ram 4C 6 (3E 37)
Cottage Row CT13: S'wch 4B 48
Cottington La. CT12: C'snd 4D 34
Cottington Link CT12: C'snd 4D 34
Cottington Rd. CT12: C'snd, Ram 4C 34
Cotton M. CT5: Swale 3C 16
Cotton Rd. CT1: Cant 3D 42
Coulter Rd. CT6: H Bay 3H 17
Countess Mountbatten Ct. CT8: Wgte S 5A 10
County Court
Thanet 3F 7 (3G 11)
Courtlands CT6: H Bay 3F 19
Courtlands Ct. CT12: C'snd 4G 35
Courtlands Way CT8: Wgte S 4B 10
Court Mt. CT7: Birch 1E 25
Court Rd. CT7: St N 4D 22
Courts, The CT9: Mgte 4C 10
Court St. ME13: Fav 3F 47
Covell's Row CT9: Mgte 4F 7 (3G 11)
Coventina Ho. CT11: Ram 2A 6
Coventon La. CT13: S'wch 6B 48
Coventry Gdns. CT6: Belt 2H 19
Cowdrey Pl. CT1: Cant 4H 43
Cow La. CT1: Cant 3D 42
Cowley Ri. CT9: Mgte 5C 12
Cowper Cl. CT5: Swale 2D 16
Cowper Rd. CT9: Mgte 5G 7 (4H 11)
Coxes Av. CT12: Ram 4B 28
Coxes La. CT12: Ram 4B 28
Coxett Hill ME13: Osp 6A 46
Craddock Dr. CT1: Cant 1H 43
Craddock Ho. CT1: Cant 1H 43
Craddock Rd. CT1: Cant 1H 43
Crampton Ct. CT10: B'stairs 3G 29
Crampton Tower Mus. 3G 29
Cranborne Wlk. CT1: Cant 5E 39
Cranbourne Cl. CT11: Ram 1F 37
Cranbrook Cl. CT9: Clift 4E 13
Cranleigh Cl. CT5: Whit 5G 15
Cranleigh Gdns. CT5: Whit 5G 15
Cranmer Cl. CT4: Bek 6F 45
Cranmer Ho. CT2: Cant 1D 42
Craven Cl. CT9: Garl 5E 11

Crawford Gdns. CT9: Mgte 3B 12
Crawford Rd. CT10: St Pet 2F 29
Creighton Flats *CT13: S'wch* 4B 48
(off School Rd.)
Creine Mill La. Nth. CT1: Cant 4A 4 (2E 43)
Cremer Pl. ME13: Fav 3C 46
Crescent, The CT1: Cant 6C 4
CT2: Cant 5F 39
CT5: Whit 5A 16
Crescent Ho. CT9: Mgte 3H 7
Crescent Rd. CT7: Birch 6E 9
CT9: Mgte 3F 11
CT10: B'stairs 5H 13
CT11: Ram 4A 6 (2C 36)
ME13: Fav 4F 47
Cress Way ME13: Fav 4C 46
Cresta Cl. CT6: H Bay 1F 17
Cricketers, The CT10: B'stairs 5E 29
Crinan Ct. CT11: Ram 6F 29
Crispe Pk. Cl. CT7: Birch 6F 9
Crispe Rd. CT7: Acol 2C 24
Crispin Cl. ME13: Fav 3F 47
Crofton Rd. CT8: Wgte S 4A 10
Croft's Pl. CT10: B'stairs 3H 29
Cromwell Rd. CT1: Cant 4G 43
CT5: Whit 3F 15
Cross La. ME13: Fav 4E 47
Crossley Av. CT6: H Bay 1F 17
Cross Rd. CT7: Birch 5E 9
Cross St. CT2: Cant 1E 43
CT6: H Bay .4B 18
Crossways CT2: Cant 4F 39
Crossways Av. CT9: Mgte 2A 28
Crow Hill CT10: B'stairs 2H 29
Crow Hill Rd. CT9: Garl 5D 10
Crown Gdns. CT2: Cant 1E 43
Crown Hill Rd. CT6: H Bay 3A 18
Crundale Way CT9: CT13: S'wch . . . .
Crystal Bus. Cen. CT13: S'wch 3D 48
Cudham Gdns. CT9: Clift . . . .
Culpepper Cl. CT2: Cant 4G 39
Culvert, The CT6: H Bay 2D 18
Cumberland Av. CT1: Cant 3B 44
CT10: B'stairs 2G 29
Cumberland Rd. CT9: Clift 2B 12
CT11: Ram .3D 36
Cundishall Cl. CT5: Whit 5E 15
Cunningham Cres. CT7: Birch 6C 8
Curlew Cl. CT6: Broom 5G 19
Curlinge Ct. CT11: Ram 3A 36
Curtis Way ME13: Fav 4A 6
Curzon Ho. CT11: Ram . . . .
Cushings Wlk. *CT5: Whit* 3F 15
(off Island Wall)
Cushman Rd. CT1: Cant 3E 43
Cuthbert Rd. CT8: Wgte S 5H 9
Cuttings, The CT12: Ram 1C 36
Cypress Cl. CT5: Whit 6E 15
Cyprus Rd. ME13: Fav 4G 47

D

Daigor La. CT12: Mans 6F 27
Daimler Av. CT6: H Bay 2H 17
Dalby Rd. CT9: Mgte 2H 7 (2A 12)
Dalby Sq. CT9: Clift 2H 7 (2A 12)
Dallinger Rd. CT7: Birch 5D 8
Dalloway CT2: Cant 3E 39
Dalmally Vs. CT2: B Oak 3B 40
Dalmaney Cl. CT10: B'stairs 2H 29
Dalmeny Av. CT9: Mgte 4D 12
Dalton Ct. CT11: Ram 3C 6
Damerham Cl. CT2: Cant 5E 39
Dan Dr. ME13: Fav 3C 46
Dane Ct. Gdns. CT10: B'stairs 2D 28
Dane Ct. Rd. CT10: B'stairs 6C 12
Dane Cres. CT11: Ram 1B 6 (1E 37)
Dane End Rd. CT8: Wgte S 5H 9
Dane Gdns. CT9: Mgte 5C 12
Dane Hill CT9: Mgte 3G 7 (2H 11)
Dane Hill Gro. CT9: Mgte 3G 7 (3H 11)
Dane Hill Row CT9: Mgte 2H 7 (3H 11)
Danehurst CT8: Wgte S 4A 10
Dane John CT1: Cant 6C 4 (3F 43)
Dane John Cotts. CT1: Cant 3F 43
Dane John Ct. CT1: Cant 6C 4 (3F 43)
Dane John Gdns. 6C 4 (3F 43)
Dane John M. CT1: Cant 2A 44
Dane John Mound 6C 4
Dane John Wlk. CT1: Cant 6C 4 (3F 43)
Dane Mt. CT9: Mgte 5C 12
Dane Pk. Rd. CT9: Mgte 3H 7 (3H 11)
CT11: Ram 1C 6 (1E 37)
Dane Pk. Vs. CT9: Mgte 3H 7
Dane Ri. CT9: Mgte 5C 12

Dane Rd. CT7: Birch . . . . .1H 23 & 6A 8
CT9: Mgte 3H 7 (3H 11)
CT11: Ram 1C 6 (1E 37)
Danesmead Ter. CT9: Mgte 3H 7 (3H 11)
Dane Valley Rd. CT9: Mgte 4B 12
CT10: St Pet 6D 12
Daniels Ct. CT5: Whit 4E 15
Darenth Cl. CT6: Hern 4F 19
Dargate Rd. CT5: Seas, York 4C 30
Dark Hill ME13: Fav 3D 46
Darnley Cl. CT10: B'stairs 4F 29
Darrell Cl. CT6: H Bay 4A 18
Darren Gdns. CT10: B'stairs 5F 29
Darwin College CT2: Cant 3E 39
Darwin Rd. CT2: Cant 5D 8
CT7: Birch .6A 8
Daryngton Av. CT7: Birch 6A 8
David Av. CT9: Clift 3D 12
David's Cl. CT10: B'stairs 4H 29
Davidson Rd. CT2: Cant 1D 42
DAVINGTON 3E 47
Davington Cotts. ME13: Fav 3E 47
Davington Hill ME13: Fav 3E 47
Dawsons Row ME13: Osp 5C 46
Daytona Way CT6: H Bay 1G 17
Deal Rd. CT13: S'wch, Worth 6B 48
Dean Ct. CT1: Cant 1G 5 (1G 43)
CT5: Whit 4G 15
Dean Cft. CT6: Broom 5F 19
Deane Cl. CT5: Whit 6G 15
CT6: H Bay .1F 43
Deans Mill Ct. CT1: Cant 1F 43
Deansway Av. CT2: Sturry 1C 40
Deborah Cl. CT5: Whit 6H 15
De Havillands CT4: Bek 6H 45
Delacourt Cl. CT12: C'snd 4E 35
Delaware Cl. CT2: Sturry 2D 40
Delfside CT13: S'wch 5C 48
Delf St. CT13: S'wch 4B 48
Delmar Cl. CT5: Swale 2D 16
Denbigh Rd. CT12: Ram 6A 28
Dence Cl. CT6: H Bay 2F 19
Dence Pk. CT6: H Bay 3F 19
Dene, The CT1: Cant 5H 43
Dene Wlk. CT9: Mgte 6H 11
Dengrove Pk. CT2: B Oak 2B 40
Denmark Rd. CT11: Ram 2C 6 (1E 37)
Denne Cl. CT2: Sturry 1D 40
Denstead Ct. CT2: Cant 4C 38
DENT-DE-LION 5C 10
Dent-de-Lion Ct. CT9: Garl 5C 10
Dent-de-Lion Rd. CT8: Wgte S 4A 10
CT9: Garl 5B 10
Denton Way CT9: Mgte 4C 12
Dering Rd. CT6: H Bay 3D 18
Derwent Av. CT11: Ram 2A 36
Desmond Cres. ME13: Fav 6H 47
D'este Rd. CT11: Ram 2F 37
Detling Av. CT10: B'stairs 6G 29
Devon Gdns. CT7: Birch 1D 24
Devon Rd. CT1: Cant 2B 44
Devonshire Gdns. CT9: Clift 3B 12
Devonshire Ter. CT10: B'stairs 2H 29
Dextor Cl. CT2: Cant 6F 39
Diamond Ho. *CT5: Whit* 3G 15
(off Diamond Rd.)
Diamond Rd. CT5: Whit 3G 15
Dickens Av. CT1: Cant 6A 40
Dickens House Mus. 3H 29
Dickens Rd. CT10: B'stairs 2H 29
Dickens Wlk. *CT10: B'stairs* 3H 29
(off Albion St.)
Dilnot La. CT7: Acol 4F 25
Discovery Pk. Ent. Zone CT13: S'wch 1C 48
Discovery Wlk. CT1: Cant 3A 44
Doggerel Acre CT5: Whit 6H 15
Dolphin Cl. CT10: B'stairs 3G 13
Dolphin Ct. CT6: H Bay 2C 18
Dolphin St. CT6: H Bay 2C 18
Dominic Ct. *CT10: St Pet* 2E 29
(off Tippledore La.)
Domneva Rd. CT8: Wgte S 5H 9
CT12: Minst .3F 33
Donegal Rd. CT1: Cant 2A 44
Donnahay Rd. CT12: Ram 4C 28
Donnithorne Ho. *CT6: H Bay* 2C 18
(off Brunswick Sq.)
Donsway Dr. CT1: Cant 1D 4 (1F 43)
Dorcas Gdns. CT10: B'stairs 1G 29
Doric Ct. CT11: Ram 4C 36
Dormans Yd. CT11: Ram 2D 6
Dorothy Dr. CT11: Ram 5C 28
Dorset Cl. CT5: Whit 6D 14
Dorset Gdns. CT7: Birch 6D 8
Dorset Pl. ME13: Fav 4E 47
Dorset Rd. CT1: Cant 3B 44
Douglas Av. CT5: Whit 4G 15

Douglas Cl. CT10: St Pet 2E 29
Douglas Rd. CT6: H Bay 3E 19
Douro Cl. CT1: Cant 1B 44
Dove Cl. CT5: Whit 6E 15
Dove Ct. CT11: Ram 2C 6
Dovedale CT7: Birch 6F 9
Dovedale Ct. CT7: Birch 6F 9
Dover Rd. CT13: S'wch 6B 48
Dover St. CT1: Cant 5G 5 (2G 43)
Down Barton Rd. CT7: St N 6D 22
Downings, The CT6: Hern 5E 19
Downs, The *CT11: Ram* 4D 36
(off Royal Esplanade)
Downs Av. CT5: Whit 4G 15
Downs Pk. CT6: H Bay 3E 19
Downs Rd. CT2: Cant 4E 39
CT11: Ram .3A 36
Dragoon Ho. *CT1: Cant* 1G 43
(off Artillery Gdns.)
Drake Ct. CT11: Ram 1D 6
Drapers Av. CT9: Mgte 6H 7 (5H 11)
Drapers Cl. CT9: Mgte 5A 12
Drapers Homes CT9: Mgte 5A 12
Draper's Windmill 4A 12
Drive, The CT1: Cant 4H 43
CT5: Ches 5D 16
CT10: St Pet 1F 29
Droit House 2F 7 (2G 11)
Drove, The CT3: Ford 4E 41
CT5: Ches 5D 16
CT12: Monk'n 3A 32
Drovers Wlk. *CT2: Sturry* 3D 40
(off Island Rd.)
Druidstone Pk. 1A 38
Drybeck Av. CT11: Ram 2H 35
Dryden Cl. CT1: Cant 3A 44
Drying Shed La. CT1: Cant 4A 4 (2E 43)
Ducking Stool, The 2D 4
Duck La. CT1: Cant 1G 43
Dudley Av. CT8: Wgte S 5G 9
Duke St. CT9: Mgte 2F 7 (2G 11)
DUMPTON 5F 29
Dumpton Gap Rd. CT10: B'stairs 5G 29
Dumpton La. CT11: Ram 6E 29
Dumpton Pk. Dr. CT10: B'stairs 1F 37
CT11: Ram .1F 37
Dumpton Pk. Rd. CT11: Ram 1B 6 (1E 37)
Dumpton Park Station (Rail) 6F 29
Duncan Cl. CT5: Whit 6F 15
Duncan Dr. CT7: Birch 5C 8
Duncan Rd. CT5: Whit 6F 15
CT11: Ram .3D 36
Duncombe M. CT1: Cant 6H 39
Dundee Ho. CT11: Ram 4D 6
Dundonald Rd. CT10: B'stairs 3H 29
CT11: Ram .2C 36
Dunedin Rd. CT12: Ram 6A 28
Dunoon Ct. CT11: Ram 6F 29
Dunstan Av. CT8: Wgte S 6H 9
Durban Cl. CT12: Ram 6A 28
Durban Rd. CT9: Mgte 6H 7 (4A 12)
Durham Cl. CT1: Cant 4F 43
DURLOCK 4G 33
Durlock CT12: Minst 4G 33
Durlock Av. CT11: Ram 4B 36
Durnford Cl. CT2: Cant 6E 39
Durovernum Ct. CT1: Cant 3G 43
DW Fitness
Canterbury 5B 40
Thanet 3A 28
Dymchurch Ho. *CT1: Cant* 2H 43
(off St Martin's Pl.)

E

Eagle Cotts. CT11: Ram 2A 6
Eagle Hill CT11: Ram 2A 6 (2D 36)
Ealham Cl. CT4: Cant 5H 43
Earlsmead Cres. CT12: C'snd 4E 35
Eastbridge Hospital
Canterbury 2D 4 (2F 43)
Eastchurch Rd. CT9: Clift 3E 13
E. Cliff M. *CT11: Ram* 4D 6
(off Cottage Rd.)
E. Cliff Pde. CT6: H Bay 2E 19
East Cliff Prom. CT6: H Bay 2F 19
CT10: B'stairs 3H 29
EAST DUMPTON 6G 29
Eastern Esplanade CT9: Clift 2A 12
CT10: B'stairs 1H 29
Eastfield Rd. CT7: Birch 6E 9
Eastgate Cl. CT6: Hern 4F 19
East Kent CrossFit 4B 4
E. Kent Retail Pk. CT10: B'stairs 2B 28
East Kent Sports School 5B 28

EAST NORTHDOWN 4E 13
E. Northdown Cl. CT9: Clift 4E 13
East Northdown Farm Gdns. 4E 13
East Ri. CT12: Ram 6B 28
East St. CT1: Cant 5A 40
    CT6: H Bay 2E 19
    ME13: Fav 4F 47
Eaton Hill CT9: Mgte 4F 7 (3G 11)
Eaton Rd. CT9: Mgte 4E 7 (3G 11)
Ebbsfleet La. CT12: Ram 6C 34
Ebbsfleet La. Nth. CT12: Ram 4C 34
Eddie Willett Rd. CT6: H Bay 2H 17
EDDINGTON 4D 18
Eddington Bus. Pk. CT6: H Bay 4D 18
Eddington La. CT6: H Bay 4B 18
Eddington Way CT6: H Bay 4C 18
Eden Ct. CT6: H Bay 3B 18
Edenfield CT7: Birch 6F 9
Eden Rd. CT5: Seas 6C 14
Edgar Cl. CT5: Swale 2D 16
Edgar Rd. CT1: Cant 1H 43
    CT9: Clift 2A 12
    CT12: Minst 3F 33
Edgar Wlk. CT9: Clift 3A 12
Edge End Rd. CT10: B'stairs 3F 29
Edinburgh Rd. CT9: Garl 5D 10
Edinburgh Wlk. CT9: Garl 5D 10
                        (off Edinburgh Rd.)
Edith Rd. CT8: Wgte S 4B 10
    CT11: Ram 3C 36
    ME13: Fav 4C 10
Edmanson Av. CT9: Mgte 4C 10
Edward Dr. CT7: Birch 6F 9
                        (Marilyn Cres.)
    CT7: Birch 6E 9
                        (Neame Rd.)
Edward Rd. CT1: Cant 2G 43
Edward Vinson Dr. ME13: Fav 5G 47
Effingham St. CT11: Ram 4B 6 (3E 37)
Egbert Rd. CT7: Birch 5B 8
    CT8: Wgte S 4A 10
    CT12: Minst 3F 33
    ME13: Fav 5E 47
Egerton Dr. CT9: Clift 3E 13
Elder Cl. CT6: H Bay 5B 18
Elder Cotts. CT5: Broom 4H 19
Eldon Gro. CT11: Ram 3D 36
Eldon Pl. CT10: B'stairs 3H 29
Elfrida Cl. CT9: Mgte 5C 12
Elgar Bretts Ct. CT1: Cant 3F 43
Elgar Pl. CT11: Ram 2A 6 (1E 37)
Elham Cl. CT9: Mgte 4C 12
                        (off Tenterden Way)
Elham Rd. CT1: Cant 4E 43
Elham Way CT10: B'stairs 5G 29
Eliot College CT2: Cant 4E 39
Elizabeth Cl. CT6: H Bay 2D 18
    CT10: B'stairs 6H 13
Elizabeth Kemp Ct.
    CT12: Ram 6C 28
Elizabeth Rd. CT11: Ram 4D 6 (3F 37)
Elizabeth Way CT6: H Bay 4F 19
Ellen Av. CT11: Ram 6E 29
Ellenden Ct. CT2: Cant 4C 38
Ellington & Hereson School Sports Centre, The
    . . . . .5D 28
Ellington Av. CT9: Garl 5D 10
Ellington Pl. CT11: Ram 2C 36
Ellington Rd. CT11: Ram 3A 6 (2C 36)
Elliot Ct. CT1: Cant 5A 40
Elliot Ct. CT6: Belt 3G 19
Elliotts Pl. ME13: Fav 4F 47
Ellison Cl. CT5: Ches 4C 16
Ellison Ct. ME13: Fav 5G 47
Ellisons Wlk. CT1: Cant 2A 44
                        (off Kent Av.)
Ellis Rd. CT5: Tank 2A 16
Ellis Way CT6: Broom 5G 19
Elm Ct. CT8: Wgte S 5A 10
Elm Gro. CT2: Cant 5C 38
    CT8: Wgte S 5H 9
    CT12: Mans 6F 27
Elmley Way CT9: Mgte 6H 11
Elms Av. CT11: Ram 3A 6 (2D 36)
Elmstone Gdns. CT9: Clift 3E 13
Elmstone Rd. CT11: Ram 2D 36
Elm Vs. CT2: Cant 6C 38
Elmwood Av. CT10: B'stairs 5G 13
Elm Wood Cl. CT5: Swale 3C 16
Elmwood Cl. CT10: B'stairs 6F 13
Elm Wood W. CT5: Swale 3C 16
Emelina Way CT5: Whit 1D 30
Emmanuel Ho. CT9: Mgte 4G 7
Emmerson Gdns. CT5: Swale 2C 16
Emperor Ct. CT1: Cant 4C 44

Empire Cinema
    Sandwich 4B 48
Empire Ter. CT9: Mgte 5G 11
Emptage Ct. CT9: Mgte 2G 7
Ennerdale ME13: Fav 5G 47
Enterprise Rd. CT9: Mgte 1H 27
Enterprise Way CT9: Mgte 1H 27
Enticott Cl. CT5: Whit 4A 16
Epping Cl. CT6: Broom 5F 19
EPPLE 5F 9
Epple Bay Av. CT7: Birch 5E 9
Epple Bay Rd. CT7: Birch 5D 8
Epple Cotts. CT7: Birch 5F 9
Epple Rd. CT7: Birch 5F 9
Ersham Rd. CT1: Cant 3G 43
Eskdale Av. CT11: Ram 2A 36
Esmonde Dr. CT12: Mans 5B 26
Esplanade CT8: Wgte S 4G 9
Espression
    Canterbury 1F 5
Essex Av. CT6: H Bay 1H 17
Essex Gdns. CT7: Birch 1D 24
Essex Rd. CT1: Cant 3B 44
    CT8: Wgte S 5B 10
Essex St. CT5: Whit 5F 15
Estuary Cl. CT5: Swale 2E 17
Estuary Vw. Bus. Pk. CT5: Whit 2D 30
Ethelbert Cres. CT9: Clift 1H 7 (2A 12)
Ethelbert Gdns. CT9: Mgte 2H 7 (2H 11)
Ethelbert Rd. CT1: Cant 4G 43
    CT7: Birch 5B 8
    CT9: Mgte 2H 7 (2H 11)
    CT11: Ram 4A 6 (3D 36)
    ME13: Fav 5D 46
Ethelbert Sq. CT8: Wgte S 4A 10
Ethelbert Ter. CT8: Wgte S 4A 10
    CT9: Clift, Mgte 1H 7 (2H 11)
Ethelred Ct. ME13: Fav 5E 47
Ethelred Rd. CT8: Wgte S 4A 10
Ethel Rd. CT10: St Pet 2F 29
Euphrosyne CT2: Cant 3E 39
Eurokent Bus. Pk. CT12: Ram 5A 28
Evelings All. CT5: Whit 5F 15
                        (off High St.)
Everard Way ME13: Fav 3D 46
Eversleigh Ri. CT5: Whit 6H 15
Eynsford Cl. CT9: Clift 3F 13

Fairacre CT10: B'stairs 3E 29
Fairacres Cl. CT6: Belt 3G 19
Fairfax Dr. CT6: Belt 2B 20
FAIRFIELD .3D 28
Fairfield Pk. CT10: B'stairs 3E 29
Fairfield Rd. CT10: B'stairs 3E 29
    CT11: Ram 5E 29
    CT12: Minst 2F 33
Fairlawn CT5: Ches 4D 16
Fairlawn Rd. CT12: Ram 4B 28
Fairlight Av. CT12: Ram 1B 36
Fairmile Ho. CT6: H Bay 2C 18
                        (off High St.)
Fairoaks CT6: H Bay 3F 19
Fair St. CT10: B'stairs 3E 29
Fairview Cl. CT9: Mgte 3H 7 (3A 12)
Fairview Gdns. CT2: Sturry 2E 41
Fairway, The CT6: H Bay 5B 18
    ME13: Fav 5C 46
Fairway Cres. CT5: Seas 6C 14
Falala Way CT1: Cant 1H 43
Falcon M. CT11: Ram 2A 6
Farleigh Rd. CT2: Cant 5G 39
Farley Rd. CT9: Mgte 6H 11
Farm Ho. Cl. CT5: Whit 5H 15
Farrar Rd. CT7: Birch 1E 25
Farrier Cl. CT6: H Bay 4A 18
Farthings Ct. CT2: Cant 4C 38
Faulkners La. CT2: Harb 2A 42
FAVERSHAM 4F 47
FAVERSHAM COTTAGE HOSPITAL 4E 47
Faversham Ind. Est. ME13: Fav 4H 47
Faversham Pools 4E 47
Faversham Reach ME13: Fav 2F 47
Faversham Rd. CT5: Seas 6A 14
    ME13: Osp 5A 46
Faversham Station (Rail) 5F 47
Faversham Stone Chapel 4A 46
Favourite Rd. CT5: Whit 1D 30
Fellowship Wlk. CT13: S'wch 5B 48
Fenoulhet Way CT6: H Bay 2E 19
Fern Cl. CT5: Ches 4C 16
Fern Ct. CT10: B'stairs 2H 29
Ferndale Ct. CT7: Birch 1E 25
Ferndown CT7: Birch 5B 8

Fernlea Av. CT6: H Bay 3C 18
Field Av. CT1: Cant 5B 40
Fielding St. ME13: Fav 4E 47
Field Vw. CT5: Whit 6D 14
Field Way CT2: Sturry 3D 40
Fiesta Wlk. CT1: Cant 3A 44
Fife Rd. CT6: H Bay 3H 17
Fifth Av. CT9: Clift 2B 12
Fig Tree Rd. CT10: B'stairs 6F 13
Finch Cl. ME13: Fav 5F 47
Finches, The CT7: St N 5E 23
Finlay Cl. ME13: Fav 4D 46
Finsbury Ct. CT11: Ram 1B 6
Finsbury Rd. CT11: Ram 2B 6 (1E 37)
Firbank Gdns. CT9: Mgte 6F 11
Firbanks CT5: Whit 5H 15
First Av. CT9: Clift 2B 12
    CT10: B'stairs 3F 13
Fir Tree Cl. CT11: Ram 3C 36
Firtree Ct. CT2: R Comn 5A 38
Fishermans Wharf CT5: Whit 3G 15
                        (off Diamond Rd.)
Fisher Rd. CT2: Cant 1D 42
Fisher St. CT13: S'wch 4C 48
Fitzgerald Av. CT6: H Bay 4A 18
Fitzmary Av. CT9: Mgte 4C 10
Fitzroy Av. CT9: Mgte 4B 12
    CT10: B'stairs 3F 13
    CT12: Ram 5B 28
Fitzroy Rd. CT5: Tank 2H 15
Flagstaff Ct. CT1: Cant 6H 5 (3G 43)
Flamingo Dr. CT6: H Bay 5C 18
Fleets La. CT2: T Hill 1D 38
Fleetwood Av. CT6: H Bay 3B 18
Fletcher Rd. CT5: Whit 4B 16
FLETE 2F 27
Flete Rd. CT9: Mgte 3F 27
Fleur de Lis Heritage Cen. 4F 47
                        (off Preston Rd.)
Flex Appeal .2H 15
Flint Gro. CT10: St Pet 2E 29
Flood La. ME13: Fav 3E 47
Flora Rd. CT11: Ram 1C 6 (1E 37)
Florence Av. CT5: Whit 6C 14
Florence Cotts. CT11: Ram 3D 36
                        (off Coronation Rd.)
Florence Ct. CT9: Clift 2B 12
Florence Rd. CT11: Ram 3D 36
Foads Hill CT12: C'snd 3F 35
Foads La. CT12: C'snd 5F 35
Fodbury Ct. CT8: Wgte S 4A 10
                        (off Ethelbert Sq.)
Forbes Rd. ME13: Fav 5E 47
FORD 6A 20
Ford Cl. CT6: H Bay 1G 17
Ford Hills CT3: Hoath, H Bay 6A 20
    CT6: Hoath 6A 20
Fordoun Rd. CT10: St Pet 2F 29
Ford Rd. CT3: Hoath 5H 19
    CT6: Broom 5H 19
Ford Wlk. CT5: York 4C 30
FORDWICH .4E 41
Fordwich Gro. CT10: St Pet 6E 13
Fordwich Pl. CT13: S'wch 5B 48
Fordwich Rd. CT2: Sturry 3D 40
Fordwich Town Hall 4E 41
Foreland, The CT1: Cant 5H 43
Foreland Av. CT9: Mgte 3D 12
Foreland Ct. CT11: Ram 4D 36
Foreland Hgts. CT10: B'stairs 6H 13
Foreland Pk. Ho. CT10: B'stairs 6H 13
Foreness Ct. CT10: B'stairs 2G 13
Foresters Cotts. CT11: Ram 3B 6
Forge Cl. CT2: Sturry 3D 40
    ME13: Fav 5F 47
Forge La. CT5: Whit 5F 15
    CT11: Ram 2C 36
                        (off Chapel Rd.)
Forrens, The CT1: Cant 1G 5
Forrester Cl. CT1: Cant 6A 40
Fort Cres. CT9: Mgte 1G 7 (2H 11)
Fort Hill CT9: Mgte 2F 7 (2G 11)
Fort Lwr. Prom. CT9: Mgte 1G 7 (2H 11)
Fort Mt. CT9: Mgte 2H 11
Fort Paragon CT9: Mgte 1H 7 (2H 11)
Fort Prom. CT9: Mgte 1H 7 (2H 11)
                        (not continuous)
Fort Rd. CT9: Mgte 2F 7 (2H 11)
    CT10: B'stairs 2H 29
Fortuna Ct. CT11: Ram 2A 6
Forty Acres Rd. CT2: Cant 1E 43
Fostall Rd. ME13: Fav 2E 47
Foster's Av. CT10: St Pet 6E 13
Foster's Ct. CT13: S'wch 6B 48
Foundry Bus. Park, The ME13: Fav 2D 46
Fountain Inn Ct. CT9: Mgte 2F 7

Fountain St. CT5: Whit 3F 15
FOUR OAKS 3A 46
Fowler's Drove CT6: H Bay 3G 21
Foxborough La. CT12: Minst 3G 33
Foxdene Rd. CT5: Seas 1B 30
Foxdown Cl. CT2: Cant 6E 39
Foxgrove Rd. CT5: Whit 4A 16
Foxhunter Park, The CT12: Monk'n 3B 32
Fox's Cross Bottom (Local Nature Reserve)
. . . . .3C 30
Fox's Cross Hill CT5: Seas 4C 30
Fox's Cross Rd. CT5: Whit 4D 30
Frances Gdns. CT11: Ram 1F 37
Franciscan Way CT1: Cant 3C 4
Francis Rd. CT10: B'stairs 6H 13
Franklyn Ho. CT2: Sturry 3D 40
Franklyn Rd. CT2: Cant 3C 42
Frank Walters Bus. Park, The
. . . . .3D 28
Freda CT10: B'stairs 6F 29
Freeman's Cl. CT5: Seas 1C 30
Freeman's Rd. CT12: Minst 3D 32
Frencham Cl. CT2: Cant 4G 39
Freshlands CT6: Belt 1A 20
Freshwater CT2: Cant 3D 38
Freshwater Cl. CT6: H Bay 2F 21
Friars, The CT1: Cant 2C 4 (2F 43)
Friars Cl. CT5: Whit 4H 15
Friary Way CT2: Cant 6D 38
Friendly Cl. CT9: Mgte 4D 12
Friends Av. CT9: Mgte 5D 12
Friend's Gap CT9: Clift 2D 12
Frobisher Ct. CT11: Ram 1D 6
Front Brents ME13: Fav 3F 47
Frost Farm Caravan Pk. CT7: St N 5F 23
Frost La. CT7: St N 4F 23
Fulham Av. CT9: Garl 6D 10
Fullers Yd. CT9: Mgte 4G 7
Fulmar Way CT6: Belt 2B 20
Fulsam Pl. CT9: Mgte 4F 11
Fyndon Ho. CT1: Cant 3A 44

G

Gables Villas, The CT11: Ram 2C 36
(off Crescent Rd.)
Gainsborough Av. CT9: Mgte 5C 12
Gainsborough Dr. CT6: Belt 2A 20
Gainsborough Rd. CT7: Birch 5D 8
Galley Vw. CT6: H Bay 3F 21
Galliard St. CT13: S'wch 5C 48
Gallwey Av. CT7: Birch 6C 8
Gange M. ME13: Fav 4F 47
Gann Rd. CT5: Whit 3H 15
Gap, The CT1: Cant 5H 43
CT2: Blean 1A 38
Garden Cl. CT2: R Comn 6A 38
Gardeners Quay CT13: S'wch 4C 48
(off Up. Strand St.)
Garfield Pl. ME13: Fav 4F 47
Garfield Rd. CT9: Mgte 3F 11
GARLINGE 5D 10
Garrard Av. CT9: Mgte 5D 10
Gaskin Rd. ME13: Fav 4G 47
Gasoline All. CT9: Mgte 4H 7 (3H 11)
Gas Pas. CT1: Cant 6B 4 (3F 43)
Gas St. CT1: Cant 6B 4 (3F 43)
Gateacre Rd. CT5: Seas 1C 30
Gatefield La. ME13: Fav 4F 47
Gate Quays CT9: Mgte 4E 7
Gateway Ct. CT11: Ram 2F 37
(off Victoria Pde.)
Gazen Salts Nature Reserve 3B 48
Genesta Av. CT5: Whit 6D 14
Genting Casino
Margate 1H 7 (2H 11)
Geoffrey Ct. CT7: Birch 6E 9
George V Av. CT9: Mgte 5D 10
George Hill Rd. CT10: B'stairs 4E 13
George Pk. CT9: Mgte 4D 10
George Roche Rd. CT1: Cant 4F 43
Georges Av. CT5: Whit 6C 14
George Stewart Av. ME13: Fav 4A 48
George St. CT11: Ram 3B 6 (2E 37)
George Warren Ct. CT9: Mgte 5G 7 (4H 11)
Gilbert Pk. CT11: Ram 2A 6 (1D 36)
Gilbert Way CT1: Cant 4D 42
Gilchrist Av. CT6: H Bay 5A 18
Giles Gdns. CT9: Mgte 5H 11
Giles La. CT2: Cant 5C 38
Gilling Drove CT3: C'let 6A 22
(not continuous)
CT7: St N 6A 22
Gillon M. CT1: Cant 1H 43
Giraud Dr. ME13: Fav 3D 46

Gladstone Rd. CT5: Whit 3F 15
CT9: Mgte 6F 7 (4G 11)
CT10: B'stairs .4F 29
Glebe Ct. CT12: Minst 4F 33
Glebe Gdns. CT9: Garl 5D 10
Glebe Rd. CT9: Garl 5D 10
Glebe Way CT5: Whit 5F 15
Glen Av. CT6: H Bay 2G 19
Glenavon Ho. CT10: B'stairs 6H 13
(off Francis Rd.)
Glenbervie Dr. CT6: Belt 2A 20
Glenbrook Cl. CT6: Belt 2H 19
Glencoe Rd. CT9: Mgte 4A 12
Glen Iris Av. CT2: Cant 6C 38
Glen Iris Cl. CT2: Cant 6C 38
Glenside CT5: Whit 5A 16
Glenside Av. CT1: Cant 6H 39
Glen Wlk. CT5: York 4C 30
Gloucester Av. CT9: Clift 3D 12
CT10: B'stairs .4F 29
Gloucester Rd. CT5: Tank 3H 15
Godden Rd. CT2: Cant 4G 39
Godfrey Ho. CT5: Whit 5G 15
Godrevy CT2: Cant 3E 39
Godwin Rd. CT1: Cant 4C 42
CT9: Clift 3A 12
Goldcrest Wlk. CT5: Whit 1D 30
Golden Acre La. CT8: Wgte S 6H 9
Golden Cl. CT8: Wgte S 6H 9
Golden Hill CT5: Whit 6H 15
(not continuous)
Goldfinch Cl. CT6: Broom 5G 19
ME13: Fav 2E 47
Goldings Wharf ME13: Fav 3F 47
Goodwin Av. CT5: Swale 3D 16
Goodwin Ct. CT11: Ram 3D 6
Goodwin Pk. CT9: Mgte 2A 28
Goodwin Rd. CT11: Ram 3B 36
Gordon Gro. CT8: Wgte S 4A 10
Gordon Rd. CT1: Cant 3F 43
CT5: Whit 5F 15
CT6: H Bay 3D 18
CT9: Clift 2A 12
CT9: Mgte 2A 28
CT11: Ram 1A 6 (1D 36)
ME13: Fav 3G 47
Gordon Sq. CT7: Birch 6D 8
ME13: Fav 4G 47
Gore End Cl. CT7: Birch 6C 8
Gore M. CT1: Cant 6H 39
Gorrell Ct. CT5: Whit 5F 15
Gorrell Rd. CT5: Whit 4G 15
Gorse La. CT6: Broom 5G 19
Gosfield Rd. CT6: H Bay 3E 19
Gosselin St. CT5: Whit 5F 15
Goudhurst Cl. CT2: Cant 4G 39
Grafton Ri. CT6: H Bay 4A 18
Grafton Rd. CT10: St Pet 5E 13
Granary Pl. CT5: Whit 6F 15
Grand Dr. CT6: H Bay 1H 17
Grange, The CT5: Seas 1C 30
CT11: Ram 2C 36
Grange Ct. CT11: Ram 3C 36
Grange Rd. CT6: H Bay 3F 19
(not continuous)
CT10: St Pet 6F 13
CT11: Ram 2C 36
Grange Way CT10: B'stairs 5F 29
Grant Cl. CT10: St Pet 1E 29
Granville Av. CT10: B'stairs 4H 29
CT12: Ram 6B 28
Granville Cl. ME13: Fav 4E 47
Granville Ct. CT11: Ram 2F 37
(off Victoria Pde.)
Granville Dr. CT6: H Bay 3H 17
Granville Farm M. CT11: Ram 2F 37
Granville Ho. CT11: Ram 2F 37
(off Victoria Pde.)
Granville Marina CT11: Ram 2F 37
Granville Marina Ct. CT11: Ram 2F 37
(off Granville Marina)
Granville Rd. CT10: B'stairs 4H 29
Granville Theatre & Cinema 2F 37
Grasmere Av. CT11: Ram 2A 36
Grasmere Pk. CT5: Whit 5B 16
Grasmere Rd. CT5: Ches, Whit 4A 16
(not continuous)
Gravel Wlk. CT1: Cant 5E 5 (2F 43)
Graveney Rd.
ME13: Fav, Good 4H 47
Graystone Rd. CT5: Tank 2A 16
Grays Way CT1: Cant 4B 42
Great Cloisters
Canterbury Cathedral 2F 5
GREAT STONAR .1C 48
Gt. Stour M. CT1: Cant 4B 4 (2F 43)

Gt. Stour Pl. CT2: Cant 1F 43
Green, The CT2: Blean 2A 38
CT12: Mans 6F 27
Greenacres CT6: Hern 4F 19
Greenbridge Pk. CT1: Cant 4A 40
Green Cloth M. CT1: Cant 6H 39
(off Brymore Cl.)
Green Dell CT2: Cant 6E 39
Greenfield Cotts. CT1: Cant 3E 43
Greenfield Rd. CT12: Ram 5C 28
Greenfinches, The CT9: Mgte 5G 11
Greenfinches M. CT11: Ram 1A 6
Greenfinch M. CT6: H Bay 4A 18
GREENHILL 5B 18
Greenhill Bri. Rd. CT6: H Bay 4A 18
Greenhill Cl. CT12: Minst 2F 33
Greenhill Gdns. CT6: H Bay 4B 18
CT12: Minst 2F 33
Greenhill Rd. CT6: H Bay 3H 17
(not continuous)
Greenhouse La. CT2: Cant 6E 39
Green La. CT5: Whit 5F 15
CT9: Mgte 5D 12
CT10: St Pet 2E 29
Green Leas CT5: Ches 4D 16
Green Rd. CT7: Birch 5D 8
Greensole La. CT12: Mans 1G 35
Greenway ME13: Fav 3D 46
Greenwood Ind. Est. ME13: Fav 1D 46
Grenham Bay Av. CT7: Birch 5C 8
Grenham Rd. CT7: Birch 5C 8
Grenville Gdns. CT7: Birch 5C 8
Grenville Way CT10: B'stairs 3E 29
Gresham Av. CT9: Mgte 5H 11
Greyfriars 3C 4 (2F 43)
Greyfriars Cotts. CT1: Cant 4B 4 (2F 43)
Grey Friars Ct. CT10: B'stairs 4F 13
Greystones Ct. CT12: C'snd 4F 35
Grimshill Ct. CT2: Cant 4C 38
Grimshill Rd. CT5: Whit 5F 15
Grimthorpe Av. CT5: Whit 6E 15
Grinsell Hill CT12: Minst, Ram 3A 34
Grosvenor Casino
Ramsgate 3A 28
Grosvenor Gdns. CT9: Mgte 5F 7 (4G 11)
Grosvenor Hill CT9: Mgte 5F 7 (3G 11)
Grosvenor Pl. CT9: Mgte 4F 7 (3G 11)
Grosvenor Rd. CT5: Whit 6F 15
CT10: B'stairs .3G 29
CT11: Ram 2C 36
Grotto Gdns. CT9: Mgte 3H 7 (3H 11)
Grotto Hill CT9: Mgte 3H 7 (3H 11)
Grotto Rd. CT9: Mgte 3H 7 (3H 11)
Grove, The CT6: H Bay 5A 18
CT8: Wgte S 5B 10
Grove Cl. ME13: Fav 5C 46
Grove Gdns. CT9: Mgte 4E 11
Grove Pl. ME13: Fav 5C 46
Grove Rd. CT11: Ram 4A 6 (3D 36)
Grove Ter. CT1: Cant 3E 43
Grummock Av. CT11: Ram 2B 36
Grundy's Hill CT11: Ram 4B 6 (3E 37)
Guildcount La. CT13: S'wch 4B 48
Guildford Av. CT8: Wgte S 5H 9
Guildford Lawn CT11: Ram 4B 6 (3D 36)
Guildford Rd. CT1: Cant 4F 43
Guildhall Museum, The
Sandwich 4B 48
(off Cattle Mkt.)
Guildhall St. CT1: Cant 3E 5 (2F 43)
Gulbenkian Theatre 4E 39
Guy Cl. CT10: B'stairs 6G 13
Gwyn Rd. CT12: Ram 5C 28

H

Hackington Cl. CT2: Cant 4E 39
Hackington Pl. CT2: Cant 6F 39
Hackington Rd. CT2: T Hill 2E 39
Hackington Ter. CT2: Cant 6F 39
Hadleigh Gdns. CT6: H Bay 2F 19
Hadlow Dr. CT9: Clift 3E 13
HAINE 5H 27
Haine Ind. Est. CT12: Ram 6H 27
Haine Rd. CT12: Ram 3H 35
HALE 3H 23
Hales Dr. CT2: Cant 5F 39
HALES PLACE 4G 39
Halfmile Ride CT9: Mgte 6G 11
Halford Cl. CT6: Broom 5F 19
Hall by the Sea Rd. CT9: Mgte 4E 7 (3H 11)
Hallcroft Ct. CT1: Cant 2C 36
Hallett Wlk. CT1: Cant 6H 39
Hall Place Ent. Cen.
Canterbury Christ Church University . . .1B 43

Halstead Cl. CT2: Cant .4G 39
Halstead Gdns. CT9: Clift 2F 13
Halt, The CT5: Whit 6H 15
Hamels, The CT2: Sturry 3D 40
Hamill Ter. CT1: Cant 6H 39
Hamilton Cl. CT12: Ram 6A 28
Hamilton Rd. CT5: Whit .4F 15
Hampshire Rd. CT1: Cant 3B 44
HAMPTON 1H 17
Hampton Cl. CT6: H Bay 2G 17
Hampton Gdns. CT6: H Bay 2G 17
Hampton Hgts. CT6: H Bay 2A 18
Hampton Pier Av. CT6: H Bay 1H 17
Hampton Pier Yacht Club 2A 18
Ham Rd. ME13: Fav 2E 47
Ham Shades La. CT5: Whit 4A 16
Hanover Cl. CT9: Clift 3E 13
Hanover Ct. CT10: B'stairs 3F 29
Hanover Pl. CT2: Cant 6F 39
Hanover Sq. CT6: H Bay 2D 18
Hanover St. CT6: H Bay 2D 18
Hanscomb Ho. CT1: Cant 6E 39
HARBLEDOWN 2C 42
Harbledown By-Pass
  CT2: Harb, Cant, R Comn 1A 42
Harbledown Gdns. CT9: Clift 2E 13
Harbledown Pk. CT2: Harb 1C 42
Harbledown Ter. CT2: Harb 1C 42
Harbour Pde. CT11: Ram 4C 6 (3E 37)
Harbour St. CT5: Whit 3F 15
  CT10: B'stairs 3H 29
  CT11: Ram .4C 6 (3E 37)
Harbour Towers CT11: Ram 5A 6
Harcourt Dr. CT2: Cant .6D 38
  CT6: H Bay 1H 17
Hardres Rd. CT11: Ram 2C 6 (2E 37)
Hardres St. CT11: Ram 5B 6 (2E 37)
Hardy Cl. CT2: Cant 1D 42
Harebrook CT11: Ram 6F 29
Hardy Cl. CT2: Cant 6D 38
Harlequin Cl. CT6: H Bay 5C 18
Harmsworth Gdns. CT10: B'stairs 2G 29
Harnet St. CT13: S'wch .4B 48
Harold Av. CT8: Wgte S 5A 10
Harold Ct. ME13: Fav 5E 47
Harold Rd. CT7: Birch 5B 8
  CT9: Clift 3B 12
Harriets Cnr. CT5: Seas 3C 30
Harrington Cl. CT6: H Bay 4F 19
Harrison Rd. CT11: Ram 3D 36
Harrison Ter. ME13: Oare 1D 46
  (off Colegates Rd.)
Harrow Dene CT10: St Pet 2E 29
  (not continuous)
Harry Wells Rd. CT6: H Bay 2H 17
Hartsdown Leisure Cen. 4F 11
Hartsdown Pk. 5F 11
Hartsdown Rd. CT9: Mgte 4E 11
Harty Ferry Vw. CT5: Whit 1E 31
Harvest Ct. CT6: Broom 5G 19
Harvey Dr. CT5: Ches 4B 16
Harwich St. CT5: Whit 5F 15
Hassall Reach CT1: Cant 4B 42
Hastings Av. CT9: Mgte 4A 12
Hastings Pl. CT13: S'wch 5B 48
Hatch St. ME13: Fav 4E 47
Hatfeild Rd. CT9: Mgte .3E 11
Hatfield Rd. CT11: Ram 3A 6 (2D 36)
Hatherley Ct. CT9: Clift .2A 12
  (off Edgar Rd.)
Havelock St. CT1: Cant 2H 5 (2G 43)
Haven Bank CT13: S'wch 4C 48
Haven Dr. CT6: Belt 1B 20
Hawe Cl. CT2: Cant 4G 39
Hawe Farm Way CT6: Broom 5G 19
Hawes Av. CT11: Ram 6E 29
Hawk Cl. CT5: Whit 6E 15
Hawkhurst Cl. CT7: Birch 5D 8
Hawk's La. CT1: Cant 3D 4 (2F 43)
Hawkhurst Way CT10: B'stairs 5G 29
Hawks Rd. CT6: H Bay .3H 17
Hawley Sq. CT9: Mgte 4F 7 (3G 11)
Hawley St. CT9: Mgte 3F 7 (3G 11)
Hawthorn Av. CT2: Cant 6G 39
Hawthorn Cl. CT1: Cant 6E 39
HAWTHORN CORNER .4C 20
Hawthorns CT7: Wdchu .2A 26
Hawthorns, The CT10: B'stairs 3C 28
Hayes All. CT5: Whit 3F 15
  (off High St.)
Hazebrouck Rd. ME13: Fav 4E 46
Hazel Wlk. CT10: B'stairs 3C 28
Hazelwood Mdw. CT13: S'wch 6B 48
Hazlemere Dr. CT6: Belt 2H 19
Hazlemere Rd. CT5: Seas 6C 14

Headcorn Dr. CT2: Cant 4G 39
Headcorn Gdns. CT9: Clift 3E 13
Heart in Hand Rd. CT6: H Bay 5B 20
Heath, The CT5: Whit 4B 16
Heath Cl. CT2: Sturry 1D 40
Heather Cl. CT9: Mgte 5E 11
Heathwood Dr. CT11: Ram 6E 29
Heaton Rd. CT1: Cant 4E 43
Hedgend Ind. Est. CT7: St N 4F 23
Heel La. CT2: B Oak 1A 40
Heights, The CT5: Whit .6E 15
Helding Cl. CT6: Broom .5F 19
Helena Av. CT9: Mgte 6F 7 (5G 11)
Helmdon Cl. CT12: Ram 5C 28
Helter Skelter Play Cen. 3H 29
  (off York St.)
Helvellyn Av. CT11: Ram 2B 36
Hengist Av. CT9: Mgte 4B 12
Hengist Rd. CT7: Birch 6A 8
  CT8: Birch, Wgte S 5H 9
Hengist Way CT12: C'snd, Minst, Ram 1G 33
Henry Ct. CT1: Cant 3F 43
Henrys Pas. CT9: Mgte .3F 7
Herbert Pl. CT9: Mgte 4F 7 (3G 11)
Herbert Rd. CT11: Ram .3C 36
Hereford Gdns. CT7: Birch 1D 24
HERESON 2E 37
Hereson Rd. CT11: Ram 2D 6 (1F 37)
Hereward Av. CT7: Birch 5C 8
Heritage Cl. CT5: Seas .1C 30
Heritage Ct. CT1: Cant .4D 4
Heritage Ho. CT1: Cant .5D 4
HERNE 6E 19
Herne Av. CT6: H Bay 4E 19
HERNE BAY 2D 18
Herne Bay Amateur Rowing Club 2A 18
Herne Bay Angling 2A 18
Herne Bay Clock Tower .2D 18
Herne Bay Golf Course .5D 18
Herne Bay Golf Driving Range 5B 18
Herne Bay Hippodrome .3D 18
  (off Kings Rd.)
Herne Bay Little Theatre 3C 18
Herne Bay Mus. & Gallery 2D 18
Herne Bay Pier 2C 18
Herne Bay Rd. CT2: Sturry 1C 40
  CT3: Sturry 1C 40
  CT5: Swale, Tank 2B 16
Herne Bay Sailing Club .2E 19
Herne Bay Station (Rail) 4C 18
Herne Bay W. Ind. Est.
  CT6: H Bay 4A 18
Herne Bus. Pk. CT6: Hern 5E 19
Herne Ct. CT6: H Bay 2D 18
Herne Dr. CT6: H Bay 5A 18
Herne St. CT6: Hern 6E 19
Herneville Gdns. CT6: H Bay 3F 19
Herne Windmill 5E 19
Herons Leisure Cen. 2D 18
Herschell Rd. CT7: Birch 5D 8
Hertford Ct. CT1: Cant 2A 44
Hertford Ho. CT11: Ram .5B 6
  (off Hertford Pl.)
Hertford Pl. CT11: Ram 5B 6 (3E 37)
Hertford Rd. CT9: Mgte .5C 12
Hertford St. CT11: Ram 5A 6 (3D 36)
Hever Pl. CT2: Cant 5G 39
Heywood M. CT1: Cant .1H 43
Hibernia St.
  CT11: Ram .4C 6 (3E 37)
Hidden Mdw. ME13: Fav 4D 46
Highbury Gdns. CT12: Ram 4B 28
Highbury Wlk. CT12: Ram 5B 28
Highfield Bus. Cen. CT1: Cant 3E 43
Highfield Cl. CT2: Blean .5B 38
  CT12: Ram 4B 28
Highfield Ct. CT6: H Bay 3C 18
  CT12: Ram 5B 28
Highfield Gdns. CT9: Mgte 4F 11
Highfield Rd. CT12: Ram 4B 28
Highfields Av. CT6: Belt .3G 19
Highfields Vw. CT6: Belt 3G 19
Highgate Rd. CT5: Whit .4B 16
Highlands Glade CT12: Mans 6G 27
HIGHSTEAD 6C 20
Highstead La. CT3: C'let, Hoath 6B 20
HIGHSTREET 5A 30
High St. CT1: Cant 2D 4 (2F 43)
  CT2: Ford 4E 41
  CT2: Sturry 3D 40
  CT5: Whit 3F 15
  CT6: H Bay 2C 18
  CT9: Garl 1D 26
  CT9: Mgte 3F 7 (3G 11)
  CT10: B'stairs 3G 29
  CT10: St Pet 2E 29

High St. CT11: Ram 2B 36
  (Nethercourt Farm Rd.)
  CT11: Ram 2A 6 (2D 36)
  (St Clements Ct.)
  CT12: Mans 1E 35
  CT12: Minst 3G 33
  CT13: S'wch 4C 48
Highstreet Rd. ME13: Darg, Hernh 5A 30
  (not continuous)
High St. St Gregory's CT1: Cant 1G 43
High Vw. Av. CT6: H Bay 1H 17
Hilary Cl. CT6: H Bay 3G 19
Hildersham Cl. CT10: St Pet 2E 29
HILLBOROUGH 3B 20
Hillborough Bus. Pk. CT6: H Bay 3B 20
Hillborough Dr. CT6: Belt 1B 20
Hillborough Rd. CT6: H Bay 2F 19
Hillbrow Av. CT2: Sturry .1D 40
  CT6: Hern 5F 19
Hillbrow Rd. CT11: Ram .1D 36
Hillcrest Gdns. CT11: Ram 3B 36
Hillcroft Rd. CT6: Hern 4F 19
Hiller Cl. CT10: B'stairs .1G 29
Hill Ho. Dr. CT12: Minst .2G 33
Hillman Av. CT6: H Bay .1G 17
Hillside Av. CT2: Cant 1C 42
Hillside Rd. CT5: Whit 4A 16
Hillside Ter. ME13: Fav 4E 47
  (off South Rd.)
Hilltop CT5: Whit 6F 15
Hill Top Rd. CT6: H Bay .2F 19
Hillview CT9: Mgte 6F 11
Hillview Rd. CT2: Cant 6C 38
  CT5: Whit 5F 15
Hilton Cl. ME13: Fav 5F 47
Hinchliffe Way CT9: Mgte 5D 12
HMP Canterbury CT1: Cant 2H 43
Hoades Wood Rd. CT2: Sturry 1E 41
Hoath Rd. CT2: Sturry 1F 41
  CT3: Hoath, Sturry 1F 41
Hobart Rd. CT12: Ram 6A 28
Hockeredge Gdns. CT8: Wgte S 5B 10
Hockley Vs. CT9: Mgte 5G 7
Hode La. CT4: Brid 6C 44
Hodges Gap CT9: Clift 2C 12
Hodges Gap Prom. CT9: Clift 2C 12
Hodgson Rd. CT5: Seas .6A 14
Hogarth Ct. CT2: Cant 3E 39
Hogarth Cl. CT6: Belt 2A 20
Holbrook Dr. CT12: Ram .6B 28
Holiday Sq. CT9: Mgte 2F 7 (2G 11)
Holland Cl. CT10: B'stairs 3G 13
HOLLICONDANE 6D 28
Hollicondane Rd. CT11: Ram 1A 6 (1D 36)
Hollow La. CT1: Cant 4E 43
Hollowmede CT1: Cant 4E 43
Hollowshore Cruising Club 1D 46
Holly Cl. CT10: B'stairs .3C 28
Holly Gdns. CT9: Mgte 3C 12
Holly La. CT9: Mgte 3C 12
Holly Rd. CT11: Ram 1B 6 (1E 37)
Holman M. CT1: Cant 6F 5 (3G 43)
Holmes Ct. CT1: Cant 1H 43
  (off College Rd.)
Holmes Way CT12: Ram .4A 28
Holm Oak Cl. CT1: Cant .4F 43
Holm Oak Gdns. CT10: B'stairs 3F 29
Holmscroft Rd. CT6: Belt 2H 19
Holters M. CT1: Cant 4H 5
Holters Mill CT2: Cant 6F 39
Holton Cl. CT7: Birch 1E 25
Holy Ghost All. CT13: S'wch 4C 48
  (off High St.)
Homefern Ho. CT9: Mgte 2G 7
Homefleet Ho. CT11: Ram 3D 6
Homeleigh Rd. CT12: Ram 4B 28
Homersham CT1: Cant 4D 42
Homespire Ho. CT1: Cant 1G 43
  (off Knotts La.)
Homestall Ct. CT2: Cant .4C 38
Homestead Cl. CT9: Mgte 6H 7 (4H 11)
Homestead Village CT11: Ram 3C 36
Homewood Rd. CT2: Sturry 2E 41
Homing Pk. CT5: Seas 2C 30
Honey Hill CT5: Whit 6G 31
Honeysuckle Cl. CT9: Mgte 5E 11
Honeysuckle Ct. CT11: Ram 1D 6 (1F 37)
Honeysuckle Way CT6: Broom 5H 19
Honeywood Cl. CT1: Cant 6H 39
Honfleur Rd. CT13: S'wch 5B 48
HOO 3C 32
Hoopers La. CT6: Broom 5H 19
Hopes La. CT12: Ram 4C 28
Hopeville Av. CT10: St Pet 1D 28
Hop Gdn. Cotts. CT1: Cant 4E 43

Hop Gdn. Way CT1: Cant 4E 43
   (off Elham Rd.)
Hornby Vis. Cen. 1A 28
Hornet Cl. CT10: B'stairs 4D 28
Horsa Rd. CT7: Birch 6B 8
Horsebridge Arts & Community Cen. 3F 15
   (off Horsebridge Rd.)
Horsebridge Rd. CT5: Whit 3F 15
Horseshoe M. CT1: Cant 3E 43
   (off Tudor Rd.)
Horsford Wlk. ME13: Fav 3C 46
Horshams, The CT6: Belt 2H 19
HORTON 6A 42
Hoser Gdns. CT7: Birch .6E 9
Hospital La. CT1: Cant 4C 4 (2F 43)
Hothe Ct. CT2: Cant 4C 38
Hovenden Cl. CT2: Cant 4G 39
Howard Rd. CT10: B'stairs 4G 29
Howland M. CT1: Cant 4E 43
Howletts Wild Animal Pk. 3H 45
Hoystings Close, The CT1: Cant 3G 43
Hubart Pl. CT2: Sturry 3D 40
Hubert Way CT10: St Pet 1E 29
Hudson Cl. CT2: Sturry 2D 40
Hudson Rd. CT1: Cant 6H 39
Hugh Pl. ME13: Fav 4F 47
   (off Leslie Smith Dr.)
Hugin Av. CT10: St Pet .6E 13
Humber Av. CT6: H Bay 1F 17
Hundreds Cl. CT8: Wgte S 6H 9
Hunters Chase CT5: Whit 6G 15
   CT6: Broom 5G 19
HUNTERS FORSTAL 5F 19
Hunters Forstal Rd. CT6: Broom 5F 19
Hunting Ga. CT7: Birch 5D 8
Hunton Gdns. CT2: Cant 4G 39
Hurst Gro. CT12: Ram .6C 28
Hythe Pl. CT13: S'wch 5B 48

I

Ibis Cl. CT5: Whit 1D 30
Iffin La. CT4: Cant 6E 43
Ince Rd. CT2: Sturry 1D 40
Infirmary (remains of)
   Canterbury 2G 5
Ingle Cl. CT7: Birch 6F 9
Ingoldsby Rd. CT1: Cant 4D 42
   CT7: Birch 6B 8
Institute Rd. ME13: Fav 4F 47
Inverary Ct. CT11: Ram 6E 29
Inverness Ter. CT10: B'stairs 4G 29
Invicta Cl. CT1: Cant .4H 43
   CT9: Mgte 4B 12
Invicta Ho. CT1: Cant .3F 43
   CT9: Mgte 4B 12
Invicta Rd. CT5: Whit .5H 15
   CT9: Mgte 5B 12
Invicta Way CT12: Mans 6G 25
Irchester St. CT11: Ram 3D 6
Irchester Vs. CT11: Ram 3D 6
Iron Ct. CT1: Cant 3F 5 (2G 43)
Iron Wharf ME13: Fav .2G 47
Irvine Dr. CT9: Mgte 5C 12
Irvine M. CT9: Mgte 5C 12
Island Rd. CT2: Sturry, West 3D 40
Island Wall CT5: Whit .4E 15
Italianate Greenhouse 6G 29
Ivanhoe Rd. CT6: H Bay 4E 19
   CT8: Wgte S 4A 10
Ives Ga. CT13: S'wch .4C 48
Ivory Cl. ME13: Fav 2C 46
Ivychurch Gdns. CT9: Clift 3E 13
Ivy Cott. Hill CT12: Minst 2A 34
Ivy Ct. CT2: T Hill 2E 39
Ivy Ho. Rd. CT5: Whit .4H 15
Ivy La. CT1: Cant 5H 5 (2G 43)
   CT11: Ram 3D 36
Ivy Pl. CT1: Cant 3E 43

J

Jackson Rd. CT1: Cant 3E 43
Jackson's Stables CT8: Wgte S 4B 10
   (off Station Rd.)
Jacob Ct. CT2: Cant 3E 39
Jacob Cl. CT9: Mgte 6G 11
Jacob Yd. ME13: Fav .4F 47
   (off Preston St.)
Jaffa Ct. CT5: Whit 5F 15
James Ct. CT9: Clift 3B 12
James St. CT11: Ram 5A 6 (3D 36)
Jane Grn. M. CT1: Cant 6H 39
Jardins Cl. CT11: Ram 2A 6 (2D 36)
Jarretts Yd. CT9: Mgte 4H 7 (3H 11)

Jayne Wlk. CT5: Whit .1D 30
Jennifer Gdns. CT9: Mgte 5C 12
Jessica M. CT1: Cant .1H 43
Jesuit Cl. CT2: Cant 4G 39
Jesus Hospital CT1: Cant 1G 43
   (off Starle Cl.)
Jewry La. CT1: Cant 3D 4 (2F 43)
John Anderson Ct. ME13: Fav 4F 47
   (off East St.)
John Goldfinch Ct. ME13: Fav 4B 46
John Graham Ct. CT1: Cant 1D 46
John Hall Cl. ME13: Fav 1D 46
John Nicholas Ho. CT11: Ram 5A 6
John's Grn. CT13: S'wch 6A 48
John St. CT10: B'stairs 3H 29
John Townsend M. CT9: Mgte 5H 7 (4A 12)
John Wilson Bus. Pk. CT5: Ches 4B 16
Joseph Conrad Ho. CT2: Cant 1D 42
Joseph Wilson Ind. Est. CT5: Whit 6A 16
Joss Gap Rd. CT10: B'stairs 4H 13
Joy La. CT5: Whit 6C 14
Jubilee Cotts. CT2: Ford 4D 40
Jubilee Ct. CT1: Cant .3E 43
   (off Wincheap)
   CT10: B'stairs 3H 29
   (off Oscar Rd.)
   CT11: Ram 2F 37
   (off Albion Rd.)
Jubilee Rd. CT13: S'wch 5B 48
Jubilee Way ME13: Fav 5G 47
Judd Rd. ME13: Fav 4C 46
Julie Cl. CT10: B'stairs 1G 29
Junction Rd. CT6: H Bay 5A 18
Jungle Jim's
   Birchington 2F 25
Juniper Cl. CT1: Cant .4G 43
   CT5: Whit 4H 15
Jutes La. CT12: Ram 6C 34

K

Kathryns Ct. CT6: H Bay 3D 18
   (off Park Rd.)
Kavanagh Cinema 2D 18
   (off William St.)
Keat Farm Cl. CT6: Belt 2B 20
Keats Cnr. CT1: Cant .2F 35
Keats Pl. CT9: Mgte 5H 7 (4H 11)
Keith Av. CT12: Ram 1A 36
Kemp All. CT5: Whit 4F 15
   (off Middle Wall)
Kemp Rd. CT5: Swale .3C 16
Kemsdale Ct. CT2: Cant 4C 38
Kemsing Gdns. CT2: Cant 4H 39
Kendal Cl. CT11: Ram .3A 36
Kendal Mdw. CT5: Ches 4E 17
Kendal Ri. CT10: B'stairs 2G 29
Kennedy Cl. ME13: Fav 3D 6
Kennedy Ho. CT11: Ram 3D 6
Kensington Rd. CT1: Cant 4A 40
KENT & CANTERBURY HOSPITAL 5G 43
Kent Av. CT1: Cant 2A 44
Kent CC Club 4H 43
Kent Gdns. CT7: Birch .6D 8
Kent Innovation Cen. CT10: B'stairs 3C 28
Kentmere Av. CT11: Ram 2H 35
Kenton Gdns. CT12: Minst 3F 33
Kent Pl. CT11: Ram 4D 6 (3F 37)
Kent Rd. CT9: Mgte 5B 12
Kent St. CT5: Whit 5F 15
Kent Ter. CT11: Ram 4D 6 (3F 37)
Keynes College CT2: Cant 5D 38
Keyworth M. CT1: Cant 6H 39
Kilbride Ct. CT11: Ram 6F 29
Kiln Ct. CT1: Cant 5A 40
   ME13: Fav 4C 46
Kilndown Gdns. CT2: Cant 4G 39
   CT9: Clift 3E 13
Kimberley Cl. CT8: Wgte S 4A 10
   (off Egbert Rd.)
Kimberley Gro. CT5: Seas 1B 30
Kimberley Rd. CT12: Ram 6A 28
King Arthur Rd. CT12: C'snd 1A 36
King Charles Av. CT12: Ram 1A 36
King Edward Av. CT6: H Bay 3F 19
   CT10: B'stairs 3G 29
King Edward Ct. CT6: H Bay 3F 19
King Edward Rd. CT7: Birch 1D 24
   CT11: Ram 3C 36
King Edward St. CT5: Whit 4F 15
Kingfisher Cl. CT5: Whit 6E 15
   CT9: Garl 5D 10
Kingfisher Ct. CT6: H Bay 4B 18

Kingfisher Wlk. CT10: St Pet 2F 29
Kings Av. CT5: Whit 4G 15
   CT7: Birch 5B 8
   CT10: B'stairs 2H 29
   CT12: Ram 6B 28
Kingsbridge Apartments, The CT1: Cant 2D 4
KINGSDOWN PARK 2H 15
Kingsdown Pk. (East) CT5: Tank 3H 15
Kingsdown Pk. (West) CT5: Tank 3H 15
Kingsfield Rd. CT6: Broom 5F 19
KINGSGATE 4F 13
Kingsgate Av. CT10: B'stairs 4F 13
Kingsgate Bay Rd. CT10: B'stairs 3H 13
Kingsgate Castle CT10: B'stairs 4H 13
Kings Hall, The
   Herne Bay 2E 19
Kingsley Rd. CT5: Whit 5G 15
Kingsmead Leisure Cen. 6G 39
Kingsmead Rd. CT1: Cant 6G 39
   CT2: Cant 6G 39
Kings M. CT1: Cant 1G 43
   CT9: Mgte .2G 7 (2H 11)
   CT11: Ram 3D 36
   (off Coronation Rd.)
Kingsnorth Rd. ME13: Fav 5E 47
Kings Pk. CT1: Cant 1H 43
Kings Pl. CT11: Ram 4C 6
Kings Rd. CT6: H Bay .2D 18
   CT7: Birch 1E 25
   CT11: Ram 1A 6 (1D 36)
   ME13: Fav 4E 47
King's School Art Centre, The 1D 4
King's School Recreation Centre, The 6F 39
King's Theatre
   Ramsgate 4C 6
Kingston Av. CT9: Garl .6D 10
Kingston Cl. CT6: Belt .2B 20
   CT12: Ram 5B 28
King St. CT1: Cant 1E 5 (1F 43)
   CT2: Ford 4D 40
   CT9: Mgte .2F 7 (2G 11)
   CT11: Ram 4C 6 (2E 37)
   CT13: S'wch 4C 48
Kingswood Hgts. CT11: Ram 3B 6
Kingswood Rd. CT11: Ram 4B 6
Kirby's La. CT2: Cant .1F 43
Kirkstone Av. CT11: Ram 2H 35
Kite Farm CT5: Swale .2D 16
Kittiwake Cl. CT6: Belt 2B 20
Knight Av. CT2: Cant 2C 42
Knightrider St. CT13: S'wch 5C 48
Knights All. CT5: Whit .3F 15
   (off High St.)
Knights Apartments, The CT1: Cant 3H 43
Knight's Av. CT10: B'stairs 1H 29
Knockholt Rd. CT9: Clift 2E 13
Knold Pk. CT9: Mgte 5G 11
Knole, The ME13: Fav .4D 44
Knots Yd. CT5: Whit 3F 15
Knotts La. CT1: Cant 1F 5 (1G 43)
Knowler Way CT6: Belt 2G 19
Knowlton Wlk. CT1: Cant 1H 43

L

La Belle Alliance Sq. CT11: Ram 3C 6 (2E 37)
   (not continuous)
Laburnum Av. CT13: S'wch 5B 4
Laburnum La. CT2: Sturry 1F 4
Lackenden Cotts. CT3: L'brne 4H 4
Ladesfield CT5: Whit 6E 1
Ladyfields CT6: Broom .5H 1
Ladysmith Gro. CT5: Seas 1B 3
   (not continuous)
Ladysmith Rd. CT5: Whit 2D 3
Ladywood Rd. CT2: Sturry 1D 4
Lady Woottons Grn. CT1: Cant 3H 5 (2G 43)
   (not continuous)
Lagos Av. CT12: Ram 6A 2
Lakeside Av. ME13: Fav 2D 4
Laking Av. CT10: B'stairs 6G 1
Laleham Gdns. CT9: Mgte 3B 1
Laleham Rd. CT9: Mgte 4B 1
Laleham Wlk. CT9: Mgte 4B 1
Lamberhurst Way CT9: Clift 2F 1
Lamberts Yd. CT10: St Pet 6D 1
Lambeth Rd. CT1: Cant 4A 4
Lambourne Wlk. CT1: Cant 2A 4
   (off Russett Rd)
Lambs Wlk. CT5: Whit .1E 3
Laming Rd. CT7: Birch .1F 2
Lammas Ga. ME13: Fav 3F 4
Lancaster Cl. CT2: Cant 6B 2
Lancaster Gdns. CT6: Belt 2H 1
   CT7: Birch 1D 1

.ancaster Rd. CT1: Cant 4F 43
.ancet Dr. CT6: H Bay 4F 19
.anchester Cl. CT6: H Bay 2G 17
.andon Rd. CT6: H Bay 2G 19
.ane End CT6: H Bay 2B 18
.ane's Wlk. CT5: Whit 3F 15
.anfranc Gdns. CT2: Harb 1C 42
.ang Ct. CT5: Swale 2C 16
.angdale Av. CT11: Ram 2A 36
.angham Cl. CT9: Mgte 4D 10
.angley Gdns. CT9: Clift 2E 13
.angton Gdns. CT1: Cant 5E 5
.angton La. CT4: Cant 6G 43
.ansdown Cotts. CT1: Cant 3G 43
.ansdown Rd. CT1: Cant 3G 43
.anthorne Rd. CT10: B'stairs 6G 13
.arch Cl. CT10: B'stairs 3D 28
.arches, The CT5: Whit 5E 15
ME13: Fav 3C 46
.arksfield Rd. ME13: Fav 2E 47
.atimer Cl. CT6: H Bay 3H 17
.aundry Rd. CT12: Minst 1G 33
.aureate Cl. CT9: Mgte 3B 12
.aurensfield CT12: Minst 2G 33
.auriston Cl. CT11: Ram 4A 36
.auriston Mt. CT10: B'stairs 2G 29
.ausanne Rd. CT9: Mgte 4G 7 (3H 11)
.ausanne Ter. CT9: Mgte 4G 7
.avender Cl. CT5: Ches 3C 16
CT9: Mgte 5E 11
.avender Gro. CT6: H Bay 3F 19
.avender La. CT12: C'snd 4E 35
.avender M. CT1: Cant 5B 4
.aw Cl. CT2: Cant 2C 42
.awn Cl. CT10: B'stairs 2G 29
.awn Rd. CT10: B'stairs 2G 29
.awns, The CT11: Ram 2D 6 (2F 37)
.awn Vs. CT11: Ram 3B 6
.awrence Gdns. CT6: H Bay 3G 19
.axton Way CT1: Cant 3A 44
CT5: Ches 4C 16
ME13: Fav 6G 47
.aylam Cl. CT10: St Pet 2D 28
.azarus Hart Havens of Rest
CT11: Ram 1D 6
.azer Rush
South Street 6A 16
.eander Ct. CT5: Tank 2A 16
.eas, The CT5: Ches 4D 16
(not continuous)
ME13: Fav 3D 46
.eas Grn. CT10: B'stairs 3D 28
.eatt Cl. CT10: B'stairs 5F 29
.ees, The CT6: Belt 2G 19
.eggetts La. CT5: Whit 3F 15
.eicester Av. CT9: Clift 3C 12
.eigh Rd. CT12: Ram 6H 27
.eighville Dr. CT6: H Bay 3B 18
.ength, The CT7: St N 5F 23
.enham Cl. CT10: B'stairs 5G 29
.enham Gdns. CT9: Garl 5D 10
.eona Ct. CT9: Mgte 3B 12
.eonards Av. CT11: Ram 6E 29
.eonie Ct. CT6: H Bay 3B 18
.eopold Rd. CT11: Ram 1B 6 (1E 37)
.eopold St.
CT11: Ram 4B 6 (3E 37)
.erryn Gdns. CT10: B'stairs 5F 13
.esley Av. CT1: Cant 4G 43
.eslie Av. CT9: Garl 6D 10
.eslie Rd. CT7: Birch 5E 9
.eslie Smith Dr. ME13: Fav 4E 47
(off South Rd.)
.es Spickett Cl. ME13: Fav 5G 47
.ewis Cl. ME13: Fav 4C 46
.ewis Cres. CT9: Garl 2B 12
.eybourne Dr. CT9: Garl 5D 10
.eybourn Rd. CT10: B'stairs 5H 29
.eycroft Cl. CT2: Cant 5E 39
.eysdown Vw. CT5: Whit 1E 31
.ibrary Rd. CT2: Cant 4E 39
.ichfield Av. CT1: Cant 4H 43
.ifeboat Station
Margate 1F 7 (2G 11)
.ilford Gallery 2E 5
.ilium Ga. CT1: Cant 5D 4
.ilian Rd. CT11: Ram 1D 6 (1F 37)
.me Gro. CT11: Ram 3D 36
(off Cannonbury Rd.)
.me Kiln Rd. CT1: Cant 3F 43
.mes Pl. ME13: Fav 4F 47
(off Preston St.)
.ncoln Av. CT1: Cant 3H 43
.ncoln Cl. CT5: Swale 2D 16
.ncoln Gdns. CT7: Birch 6D 8

Linden Av. CT5: Whit 4H 15
CT6: H Bay 3C 18
CT10: B'stairs 2H 29
Linden Chase CT2: Cant 1A 4 (1E 43)
Linden Cl. CT8: Wgte S 6A 10
Linden Gro. CT2: Cant 1A 4 (1E 43)
Linden Rd. CT8: Wgte S 5B 10
Linen Ct. CT1: Cant 5C 4
Linen Ho. CT1: Cant 5C 4
Linington Rd. CT7: Birch 1E 25
Link La. CT1: Cant 4F 5 (2G 43)
Link Rd. CT2: Sturry 2D 40
CT10: B'stairs 2D 38
CT10: St Pet 5F 13
Links, The CT6: Hern 5E 19
Links Cl. CT6: Hern 4E 19
Linksfield Rd. CT8: Wgte S 6H 9
Linley Ho. CT10: St Pet 6E 13
Linley Rd. CT10: St Pet 6E 13
Linnet Av. CT5: Whit 1D 30
Lionard Ho. CT2: Cant 1E 43
Lion Fld. ME13: Fav 4C 46
Lion Yd. ME13: Fav 5C 46
Lisa Ct. CT5: Tank 3A 16
Lismore Rd. CT5: Whit 5B 16
CT6: Belt 2H 19
Lister Ho. CT9: Mgte 5A 12
Lister Rd. CT9: Mgte 5A 12
Littlebourne Rd. CT1: Cant 2A 44
CT3: Cant 2A 44
CT4: Bek 6G 45
Lit. Charles St. CT6: H Bay 2D 18
Little Paddocks CT5: Ches 6D 16
Liverpool Lawn CT11: Ram 5B 6 (3E 37)
Livingstone Rd. CT10: St Pet 1E 29
Lloyd Rd. CT10: B'stairs 3G 29
Lodge Fld. Rd. CT5: Ches 4D 16
Lombard St. CT9: Mgte 3F 7 (2G 11)
London Rd. CT2: Cant 1D 42
CT2: Harb, Up Harb 1A 42
CT11: Ram 3B 36
ME13: Fav, Osp 4A 46
(not continuous)
Long Acre CT7: Birch 2A 26
Longacre CT5: Ches 4D 16
Long Acre Cl. CT2: Cant 6E 39
Longfield Cl. CT5: Swale 3D 16
Longfield Cl. CT5: Swale 3D 16
Longmarket CT1: Cant 3F 5 (2G 43)
Longmead Cl. CT6: H Bay 4A 18
Long Meadow CT12: Monk'n 3B 32
Long Meadow Way CT2: Cant 4F 39
Longport CT1: Cant 4H 5 (2G 43)
Longport Ho. CT1: Cant 4H 5
Long Reach Cl. CT5: Whit 1E 31
Long Rock CT5: Swale 2D 16
Longtail Ri. CT6: H Bay 5C 18
Longtye Dr. CT5: Ches 5C 16
Lonsdale Av. CT9: Clift 2B 12
Lonsdale Dr. CT6: H Bay 1H 17
Loop, The CT12: Mans 5H 25
Loop Cl. CT13: S'wch 4B 48
Loop Ct. M. CT13: S'wch 4B 48
Loop St. CT13: S'wch 4B 48
Lorina Rd. CT12: Ram 1C 36
Lorne Rd. CT11: Ram 3C 36
Loughborough Ct. CT11: Ram 2C 6
Love La. CT1: Cant 4H 5 (2G 43)
CT9: Mgte 2F 7 (2G 11)
CT13: S'wch 4C 48
(off St Peter's St.)
ME13: Fav 6H 47
Lovell Rd. CT2: R Comm 5B 38
Love St. Cl. CT6: H Bay 5A 18
Lwr. Bridge St. CT1: Cant 4G 5 (2G 43)
Lwr. Chantry La. CT1: Cant 6H 5 (2G 43)
Lwr. Herne Rd. CT6: Hern 6C 18
LOWER ISLAND 4F 15
Lwr. Northdown Av. CT9: Mgte 3B 12
Lower Rd. ME13: Bkld, Lud'm 3A 46
ME13: Fav 4C 46
Lucerne Ct. CT5: Seas 1B 30
Lucerne Dr. CT5: Seas 1B 30
Luckhurst Gdns. CT9: Clift 2E 13
LUDDENHAM 1A 46
Lullingstone Ct. CT1: Cant 5D 4
Luton Av. CT10: B'stairs 4F 29
Luton Ct. CT10: B'stairs 4F 29
Luton Rd. ME13: Fav 4G 47
LYDDEN 3G 27
Lyell Ct. CT7: Birch 5D 8
Lyell Rd. CT7: Birch 5D 8
Lyminge Way CT9: Mgte 4C 12
Lymington Rd. CT8: Wgte S 6H 9
Lyndhurst Av. CT9: Mgte 3B 12
Lyndhurst Cl. CT2: Cant 5E 39

Lyndhurst Rd. CT10: B'stairs 1G 29
CT11: Ram 2F 37
Lyngate Ct. CT9: Clift 3D 12
Lynton Pde. CT9: Clift 2A 12
(off Edgar Rd.)
Lypeatt Ct. CT2: Cant 4C 38
Lysander Ct. CT4: Bek 6H 45
CT10: B'stairs 4C 28
Lytham Av. CT6: H Bay 6B 18

M

McCarthy Av. CT2: Sturry 1D 40
Macdonald Pde. CT5: Seas 1C 30
McKinlay Ct. CT7: Birch 5B 8
(off The Parade)
Madeira Rd. CT9: Mgte 3A 12
Madeira Wlk. CT11: Ram 4C 6 (3E 37)
Magdala Rd. CT10: St Pet 1E 29
Magdalen Cl. CT1: Cant 3G 43
CT10: B'stairs 1G 29
Magistrates' Court
Canterbury 3H 5 (2G 43)
Margate 3F 7 (3G 11)
Magnolia Av. CT9: Clift 3D 12
Magnolia Ri. CT6: Broom 5H 19
Maiden La. CT1: Cant 4D 42
Maison Dieu 5C 46
Maitland Ct. ME13: Fav 2D 46
Major Cl. CT5: Whit 1D 30
Makenade Av. ME13: Fav 6F 47
Malham Dr. CT9: Mgte 4A 12
Mall, The ME13: Fav 5E 47
Mallard Cl. CT6: H Bay 5C 18
Mallory Cl. CT12: Ram 5C 28
Malthouse Rd. CT2: Cant 6F 39
Malthouses, The CT7: Birch 6D 8
Maltings, The CT1: Cant 4H 5
CT2: Cant 1E 43
(off Roper Rd.)
CT11: Ram 3A 6
ME13: Fav 3F 47
Malvern Pk. CT6: Belt 3H 19
Manciple Ct. CT2: Cant 3C 42
Mandarin La. CT6: H Bay 5C 18
Mandeville Rd. CT2: Cant 6E 39
Manktelow Ct. CT10: B'stairs 5F 29
Mannock Ho. CT1: Cant 1H 43
Manor Cl. CT1: Cant 5C 42
CT6: Belt 1B 20
Manor Ct. Flats CT1: Cant 3F 43
Manor Dr. CT7: Birch 1D 24
Manor Lea Rd. CT7: St N 6F 23
Manor Rd. CT5: Tank 2A 16
CT6: Belt 1B 20
CT7: St N 5F 23
CT10: B'stairs 3F 29
Manover Ct. ME13: Fav 3D 46
Mansions, The CT10: B'stairs 3E 29
Mansion St. CT9: Mgte 2F 7 (2G 11)
MANSTON 6F 27
MANSTON (KENT'S INTERNATIONAL AIRPORT)
..................................6D 26
Manston Bus. Cen. CT12: Monk'n 5G 25
Manston Ct. Caravan Pk.
CT12: Mans 5F 27
Manston Ct. Rd. CT9: Mgte 6E 27
CT12: Mans, Mgte 6E 27
Manston Fire Mus. 5C 26
Manston Golf Cen. 6H 27
Manston Pk. CT12: Mans 5H 25
Manston Pk. Bungs. CT12: Mans 5B 26
Manston Rd. CT12: Mans 3F 25
CT9: Mans, Mgte 4E 27
CT11: Ram 1H 35
CT12: Mans, Mgte, Ram 5C 26
Manwood Av. CT2: Cant 5F 39
Manwood Rd. CT13: S'wch 5C 48
Maple Cl. CT2: R Comm 5B 38
CT10: B'stairs 4E 13
Maple Ho. CT2: R Comm 5B 38
Maples, The CT10: B'stairs 3D 28
March Gro. CT1: Cant 1H 43
Marden Av. CT12: Ram 1B 36
Margaret Ct. CT6: H Bay 3D 18
MARGATE 3F 7 (3H 11)
Margate FC 4F 11
Margate Gallery 2F 7
Margate Harbour Arm CT9: Mgte ...2E 7 (2G 11)
Margate Hill CT7: Acol 4F 25
Margate Media Cen. CT9: Mgte 2F 7
Margate Mus. 2F 7 (2G 11)
Margate Rd. CT6: H Bay 4F 19
(not continuous)
CT10: B'stairs, Ram 3A 28

Margate Rd. CT11: Ram 1A 6 (3A 28)
  CT12: Ram 3A 28
Margate Station (Rail) 3F 11
Margate Yacht Club 2F 7
Marilyn Cres. CT7: Birch 6F 9
Marina Esplanade CT11: Ram 4D 6 (3F 37)
Marina Rd. CT11: Ram 2F 37
Marine Cres. CT5: Swale, Tank 2B 16
Marine Dr. CT9: Mgte 3E 7 (3G 11)
  CT10: B'stairs 2G 13
Marine Gap CT5: Whit 4E 15
Marine Gdns. CT9: Mgte 3E 7 (3G 11)
Marine Pde. CT5: Tank 2H 15
Mariners Ct. CT5: Whit 4F 15
Mariners Lea CT10: B'stairs 3D 28
Mariners Wlk. ME13: Oare 1D 46
Marine Studios
  Margate 3F 7
Marine Ter. CT5: Whit 3E 15
  CT9: Mgte 4E 7 (3F 11)
Maritime Av. CT6: Belt 3G 19
Mark Av. CT11: Ram 4B 36
Market Pl. CT9: Mgte 2F 7
  ME13: Fav 4F 47
Market Pl. (Sth.) CT9: Mgte 2G 11
                (off Market St.)
Market St. CT6: H Bay 2D 18
  CT9: Mgte 2F 7 (2G 11)
  CT13: S'wch .4B 48
             (not continuous)
  ME13: Fav 4F 47
Market Way CT2: Cant 6G 39
Marlborough Cl. CT10: B'stairs 4E 29
Marlborough Rd. CT5: Whit 2F 15
  CT9: Mgte 6F 7 (4G 11)
  CT11: Ram 4A 6 (3D 36)
Marley Ct. CT2: Cant 4C 38
Marlowe Arc. CT1: Cant 4E 5 (2F 43)
Marlowe Av. CT1: Cant 6D 4 (2F 43)
Marlowe Cl. CT5: Whit 4B 16
Marlowe Ct. CT1: Cant 1E 5
                (King St.)
  CT1: Cant 6D 4
           (Marlowe Av.)
Marlowe Innovation Centre, The
  CT12: Ram .5A 28
Marlowe Rd. CT9: Mgte 5C 10
Marlowe Theatre
  Canterbury 1D 4 (1F 43)
Marlowe Way CT12: Ram 5A 28
Marlow Ho. CT7: Birch 6F 9
         (off Sutherland Dr.)
Marlow Mdws. CT2: Ford 4D 40
Marrose Av. CT12: Ram 4B 28
Marshall Cres. CT10: B'stairs 3E 29
Marsham M. CT1: Cant 1H 43
           (off Starle Cl.)
Marsh Farm Rd. CT12: Minst 6F 33
MARSHSIDE 6E 21
Marshwood Cl. CT1: Cant 5A 40
Martindale Cl. CT1: Cant 3G 43
Martindown Rd. CT5: Whit 1E 31
Martin's Cl. CT12: Ram 5C 28
Martony Ct. CT9: Mgte 3H 7
MARTYRS FIELD 3E 43
Martyr's Fld. Rd. CT1: Cant 3E 43
Mary Grn. Wlk. CT1: Cant 6H 39
Maryland Gro. CT1: Cant 4H 43
Masons Ri. CT10: B'stairs 2G 29
Matador Dr. CT6: H Bay 4F 19
Matthew Ct. CT2: Cant 1F 43
Matthews Rd. CT6: H Bay 5A 18
Maugham Ct. CT5: Whit 5F 15
Maxine Gdns. CT10: St Pet 2F 29
Maxted Cl. CT6: Belt 3G 19
Maybrook Retail Pk. CT1: Cant 5A 40
Maydowns Rd. CT5: Ches 3D 16
Mayfield Rd. CT6: H Bay 4E 19
Mayforth Gdns. CT11: Ram 3B 36
Maynard & Cotton's Spital CT1: Cant 5C 4
Maynard Av. CT9: Mgte 5D 10
Maynard Rd. CT1: Cant 3D 42
May's Rd. CT11: Ram 3C 36
May St. CT6: H Bay 3B 20
Mayton La. CT2: B Oak 1B 40
Mayville Rd. CT10: St Pet 1E 29
Meadow Cl. CT6: H Bay 3G 19
Meadow Ct. CT1: Cant 6A 4
  CT9: Mgte 5B 12
         (off Dane Valley Rd.)
Meadow Dr. CT5: Ches 5D 16
Meadow Farm Caravan Pk. CT5: Swale . .2C 16
Meadow Rd. CT2: Cant 6C 38
  CT2: Sturry .2D 40
  CT9: Mgte 4D 10
Meadows, The CT6: Broom 5G 17

Meadow Vw. CT12: Monk'n 3B 32
Meadow Wlk. CT5: Whit 6E 15
Mead Way CT2: Cant 1E 43
Mecca Bingo
  Thanet 4A 28
Medina Av. CT5: Whit 6D 14
Meeting Ct. CT9: Mgte 2F 7
Meeting St. CT11: Ram 3B 6 (2E 37)
Melbourne Av. CT12: Ram 1A 36
Mellanby Cl. CT7: Birch 1E 25
Melloy M. CT9: Mgte 2G 7
Melsetter Cl. CT7: Birch 6F 9
Memel Pl. CT11: Ram 4A 6 (3D 36)
Memorial Theatre
  Broadstairs 2F 29
Mendfield St. ME13: Fav 4E 47
Mentmore Ho. CT12: Ram 4C 28
Mentmore Rd. CT12: Ram 4C 28
Mercery Ct. CT1: Cant 3E 5
Mercery La. CT1: Cant 3E 5 (2F 43)
Merchants Way CT2: Cant 3C 42
Mere Ga. CT9: Mgte 6E 7 (4G 11)
Meridian Cl. CT12: Ram 1A 36
Merlin Vs. CT9: Mgte 1H 7
Merlin Way CT12: Mans 6H 25
Merrivale Hgts. CT10: B'stairs 1A 32
Merrywood Gro. CT6: Broom 5H 19
Merton Cotts. CT1: Cant 5G 43
Merton La. CT4: Cant 6E 43
Metcalfe M. CT1: Cant 6H 39
Meteor Av. CT5: Whit 6D 14
Meverall Av. CT12: C'snd 4F 35
Mews Apartments, The
  CT1: Cant 3H 43
       (off New Dover Rd.)
Michael Av. CT11: Ram 1G 37
Michelle Gdns. CT9: Garl 5C 10
Mickleburgh Av. CT6: H Bay 4F 19
Mickleburgh Hill CT6: H Bay 3E 19
Middle Row ME13: Fav 4F 47
Middle Wall CT5: Whit 3F 15
Midlothian Cotts. CT11: Ram 1B 6
Mildmay Ct. CT11: Ram 2D 6
Miles Way CT7: Birch 6D 8
Military Rd. CT1: Cant 1H 5 (1G 43)
  CT11: Ram 6A 6 (4D 36)
Mill Cl. CT13: S'wch 3A 48
Mill Cotts. CT11: Ram 3C 36
Mill Ct. Cl. CT6: Hern 5F 19
Millennium Way CT10: B'stairs 3B 28
Miller Av. CT2: Cant 2D 42
Millers Ct. CT5: Whit 6F 15
Millers La. CT12: Monk'n 2A 32
Mill Fld. CT10: St Pet 2D 28
Millfield Mnr. CT5: Whit 4G 15
Millfield Rd. CT12: Ram 4B 28
  ME13: Fav 4G 47
Mill La. CT1: Cant 1E 5 (1F 43)
  CT2: Harb 2C 42
  CT6: Hern 6F 19
  CT7: Birch 1D 24
  CT9: Mgte 4F 7 (3G 11)
  CT12: Ram .4B 28
Mill La. (North) CT6: H Bay 4F 19
Millmead Av. CT9: Mgte 4D 12
Millmead Gdns. CT9: Mgte 4D 12
Millmead Rd. CT9: Mgte 4B 12
Mill Pl. ME13: Fav 3F 47
Mill Rd. CT2: Cant, Sturry 4C 40
Mill Row CT7: Birch 1D 24
Millstream Cl. CT5: Whit 4G 15
  ME13: Fav 4E 47
Millstrood Rd. CT5: Whit 5G 15
Mill Vw. Rd. CT6: Hern 6E 19
Mill Wall CT13: S'wch 5C 48
Millwall Pl. CT13: S'wch 5C 48
Milner Ct. CT2: Sturry 3D 40
Milner La. CT2: Sturry 3D 40
Milner Rd. CT5: Seas 1C 30
Milton Av. CT9: Mgte 5H 7 (4H 11)
Milton Cl. CT1: Cant 4A 44
Milton Rd. CT1: Cant 4G 43
Milton Sq. CT9: Mgte 5G 7
Minerva Ho. CT11: Ram 2A 6
Minnis Bay Sailing Club 6A 8
Minnis Bay Windsurfing Club 6A 8
Minnis Rd. CT7: Birch 5B 8
MINSTER 3F 33
Minster Abbey .4G 33
Minster Cl. CT10: B'stairs 5G 29
Minster Dr. CT6: H Bay 3B 18
Minster Lodge CT11: Ram 3C 36
          (off Edith Rd.)
Minster Rd. CT7: Acol, Monk'n 5F 25
  CT8: Wgte S 5A 10
  CT11: Ram .3B 36

Minster Rd. CT12: Minst, Monk'n 1G 33
  ME13: Fav 4G 47
Minster Station (Rail) 4G 33
Mint, The CT2: Harb 1C 42
Mint Yd. CT1: Cant 1F 5 (3G 43)
Moat Ho. CT1: Cant 3F 4
       (off Rhodaus Cl.)
Moat La. CT2: Ford 5D 40
  CT2: R Comn 4B 36
Moat Sole CT13: S'wch 4B 48
Mockett Dr. CT10: St Pet 6F 15
Molehill Rd. CT5: Ches 6D 16
  CT6: H Bay .6D 16
Molineux Rd. CT12: Minst 3F 33
Monastery St. CT1: Cant 4H 5 (2G 43)
Monks All. ME13: Fav 3D 46
        (off Monk's Cl.)
Monks Cl. CT2: Cant 6G 39
  ME13: Fav 3D 46
Monks Way CT13: S'wch 2B 4
MONKTON 2B 32
Monkton Cotts. CT11: Ram 3A 4
Monkton Ct. CT5: Ches 5D 16
Monkton Gdns. CT9: Clift 2E 12
Monkton Mnr. CT12: Monk'n 2A 32
Monkton Nature Reserve 1A 32
Monkton Pl. CT11: Ram 3A 6 (2D 36)
Monkton St. CT12: Minst, Monk'n 2A 32
Montague Rd. CT11: Ram 1C 6 (1E 37)
Montague St. CT6: H Bay 2C 18
Montefiore Av. CT11: Ram 6F 27
Montefiore Cotts. CT11: Ram 1D 6
Montfort Cl. CT2: Cant 4G 39
Montpelier Av. CT5: Whit 2F 31
Moorfield CT2: Cant 4F 39
Moray Av. CT7: Birch 5D 8
Mordaunt Av. CT8: Wgte S 5A 10
Morris Av. CT6: H Bay 1F 17
Mortimer St. CT5: Whit 2D 14
Moss End M. CT11: Ram 5E 28
Mount, The CT3: Cant 1D 44
  ME13: Fav 5D 46
Mount Fld. ME13: Fav 5D 46
Mountfield Way CT8: Wgte S 1H 29
Mount Grn. Av. CT12: C'snd 4F 35
MOUNT PLEASANT 1G 31
Mt. Pleasant CT2: Blean 2A 38
  ME13: Oare .1D 46
Mount Rd. CT1: Cant 4A 44
Mount Vw. Rd. CT6: Hern 5E 19
Moyes Ct. CT12: C'snd 4F 35
Muir Rd. CT11: Ram 6F 27
Mulberry Cl. CT11: Ram 1D 6 (1F 37)
Mulberry Ct. CT1: Cant 4C 4 (2F 43)
Mulberry Fld. CT13: S'wch 4B 48
Muscovy Way CT6: H Bay 4C 18
Musgrave Cl. CT12: Mans 5B 24
Mutrix Gdns. CT9: Mgte 4C 10
Mutrix Rd. CT9: Mgte 5D 10
Mutton La. ME13: Osp 6C 44
Mymms Cl. CT5: Ches 5C 16

N

Nacholt Cl. CT5: Whit 3A 14
Nackington Ct. CT1: Cant 4H 43
      (off Old Dover Rd.)
Nackington Rd. CT1: Cant 6G 43
  CT4: Cant 6G 43
Napier Rd. CT10: St Pet 1E 29
Napleton Ct. CT11: Ram 3C 36
Napleton Rd. CT11: Ram 3C 36
  ME13: Fav 4E 47
Narboths Nursery ME13: Fav 5E 47
Nash Ct. Gdns. CT9: Mgte 5G 11
Nash Ct. Rd. CT9: Mgte 5H 11
Nash Gdns. CT10: B'stairs 3H 29
Nash La. CT9: Mgte 6H 11
Nash Rd. CT9: Mgte 5G 11
Nasmyth Rd. CT7: Birch 5E 8
Naylands CT9: Mgte 4F 11
Neal's Pl. Rd. CT2: Cant 6C 38
Neame Rd. CT7: Birch 6E 8
Neighbourhood Centre, The
  Canterbury 6A 4
        (off Reed Av.)
Nelson Ct. CT7: Birch 5E 8
Nelson Cres. CT11: Ram 5B 6 (3E 37)
Nelson Gdns. ME13: Fav 5E 47
Nelson Pl. CT10: B'stairs 2H 29
Nelson Rd. CT5: Whit 4E 15
Nelson St. ME13: Fav 5E 47
Nelson Ter. ME13: Fav 5E 47
Ness, The CT1: Cant 5H 43
NETHERCOURT .2A 36

Nethercourt Circ. CT11: Ram 3B 36
Nethercourt Farm Rd. CT11: Ram 2B 36
Nethercourt Gdns. CT11: Ram 3B 36
Nethercourt Hill CT11: Ram 3B 36
Nether Court Pk. 3B 36
    (off Nethercourt Hill)
Nethercourt Touring Pk. CT11: Ram 2B 36
Netherhale Farm Rd. CT7: St N 3H 23
Nethersole Cl. CT2: Cant 4G 39
Neville Rd. CT6: Belt 3B 20
New Beverley Ho. CT2: Cant 6F 39
    (off Dextor Cl.)
Newbury Cl. CT7: Birch 1F 25
Newbys Pl. CT9: Mgte 3F 7 (3G 11)
Newcastle Hill CT11: Ram 3C 6 (2E 37)
Newce Wlk. CT1: Cant 6H 39
New Cotts. CT13: S'wch 4B 48
New Creek Rd. ME13: Fav 3G 47
New Cross St. CT9: Mgte 3F 7 (3G 11)
    CT4: Brid, Cant 3G 43
New Dover Rd. CT1: Cant 6H 5 (3G 43)
    CT4: Cant 3G 43
New Dover Road (Park & Ride) 6A 44
Newgate Gap CT9: Clift 2A 12
    (off Percy Rd.)
Newgate Lwr. Prom. CT9: Clift 1H 7 (2A 12)
Newgate Prom. CT9: Clift 1H 7 (2A 12)
New Haine Rd. CT12: Ram 4A 28
New Ho. Cl. CT4: Cant 6E 43
New Ho. La. CT4: Cant 6D 42
NEWINGTON 6A 28
    CT12: Ram 6B 28
Newington Rd. CT11: Ram 6B 28
    CT12: Ram 6B 28
Newlands Ho. CT11: Ram 5E 29
Newlands La. CT12: B'stairs 5D 28
Newlands Rd. CT12: Ram 6D 28
Newman's Cl. CT10: B'stairs 1G 29
Newport Ct. CT1: Cant 4H 43
New Rd. CT2: Up Harb, R Comn 4A 38
New Romney Pl. CT13: S'wch 5B 48
New Ruttington La. CT1: Cant 1G 43
New St. CT1: Cant .3E 43
    CT2: Cant 1E 43
    CT5: Whit 3F 15
    CT6: H Bay 2D 18
    CT9: Mgte .3F 7 (3G 11)
    CT13: S'wch 4C 48
Newton Rd. CT5: Tank 3B 16
    ME13: Fav 4F 47
New Town St. CT1: Cant 6G 39
Nicholas Dr. CT12: C'snd 4F 35
Nicholls Av. CT10: B'stairs 5F 29
Nickle Ct. CT2: Cant 4C 38
Nightingale Av. CT5: Whit 1D 30
Nightingale Pl. CT9: Mgte 3A 12
Nightingale Rd. ME13: Fav 4E 47
Nixon Av. CT12: Ram 5C 28
Nobel Cl. ME13: Fav 4D 46
Noble Ct. CT9: Garl .5C 10
Noble Gdns. CT9: Garl 5C 10
No Name St. CT13: S'wch 4B 48
Nonsuch Cl. CT1: Cant 2A 44
Nook, The CT12: Ram 4C 28
Norfolk Rd. CT1: Cant 3B 12
    CT9: Clift 3B 12
    CT9: Mgte 2F 27
Norfolk Sq. CT12: Ram 5B 28
    (off Stirling Way)
Norfolk St. CT5: Whit 5F 15
Norman Rd. CT1: Cant 3F 43
    CT5: Whit 6F 15
    CT8: Wgte S 4B 10
    CT10: St Pet 1E 29
    CT11: Ram 3B 36
    ME13: Fav 4E 47
Norman Staircase
    Canterbury 1G 5
Norrie Rd. CT7: Birch 1E 25
North Av. CT11: Ram 4A 6 (3D 36)
Northbourne Way CT9: Clift 4E 13
Northcliffe Gdns. CT10: B'stairs 6G 13
NORTHDOWN 4D 12
Northdown Av. CT9: Mgte 3B 12
Northdown Hill CT10: St Pet 5D 12
Northdown Ind. Pk. CT10: St Pet 1E 29
Northdown Pk. 4D 12
Northdown Pk. Rd. CT9: Mgte 3B 12
Northdown Rd. CT9: Mgte, Clift 2G 7 (2H 11)
    CT10: St Pet 1E 29
Northdown Trad. Est. CT10: St Pet 6D 12
Northdown Way CT9: Mgte 4C 12
Nth. Foreland Av. CT10: B'stairs 6H 13
Nth Foreland Golf Course 5G 13
Nth. Foreland Hill CT10: B'stairs 5H 13
Nth. Foreland Rd. CT10: B'stairs 6H 13
Northgate CT1: Cant 1G 43
Nth. Holmes Rd. CT1: Cant 1G 43

North La. CT2: Cant 1B 4 (1F 43)
    ME13: Fav 4E 47
North Stream CT3: M'sde 4E 21
North St. CT6: H Bay 2E 19
Northumberland Av. CT9: Clift, Mgte 3C 12
Northumberland Ct. CT9: Clift 2C 12
NORTHWOOD 4B 28
Northwood Ct. CT10: B'stairs 3C 28
Northwood Ho. CT10: B'stairs 6B 18
Northwood Rd. CT5: Tank, Whit 3G 15
    CT10: B'stairs 4C 28
    CT12: B'stairs, Ram 4C 28
Norton Dr. CT12: Minst 3F 33
Norview Rd. CT5: Whit 6D 14
Notley St. CT1: Cant 1G 43
Notley Ter. CT1: Cant 1G 43
    (off Notley St.)
Nottingham Rd. CT7: Birch 2D 24
Nunnery Flds. CT1: Cant 4G 43
Nunnery Grn. CT2: Sturry 3G 43
Nunnery Rd. CT1: Cant 3F 43
Nursery Cl. CT5: Whit 4A 16
    CT11: Ram 2C 36
Nursery Flds. CT7: Acol 4F 25
Nursery Gdns. CT10: B'stairs 4E 13
Nursery Ho. CT6: Hern 5E 19
Nursery Ind. Est. CT6: H Bay 4A 18
Nurserylands CT6: H Bay 4D 18
Nursery Wlk. CT2: Cant 6E 39

O

Oakdale Rd. CT6: H Bay 3E 19
Oakdene Rd. CT12: Ram 6C 28
Oakfield Ct. CT12: Ram 1B 36
Oakland Ct. CT6: H Bay 2C 18
    CT12: C'snd 4E 35
Oaklands Av. CT10: St Pet 2E 29
Oaklands Way CT2: Sturry 1F 41
Oakleigh La. CT4: Bek 5F 45
Oakridge CT10: B'stairs 4G 13
Oaks, The CT5: Whit 1D 30
    CT7: St N 5F 23
    CT10: St Pet 6F 13
Oaks Av. CT6: H Bay 5B 18
Oaks Pk. CT2: R Comn 5B 38
Oak Tree Gro. CT9: Garl 5C 10
Oakwood Dr. CT5: Whit 4A 16
Oakwood M. CT5: Whit 6F 15
Oakwood Rd. CT2: Sturry 1E 41
Oakwood Trad. Est. CT10: St Pet 1D 28
OARE 1C 46
Oare Gunpowder Works Country Pk. 1C 46
Oare Gunpowder Works Country Pk. Vis. Cen.
     . . . . .2C 46
Oare Meadow Nature Reserve 1D 46
Oare Rd. ME13: Fav 1D 46
Oast, The CT1: Cant 4H 43
Oast Cotts. CT1: Cant 3E 43
Oast Ct. CT9: Mgte .5H 11
Oaten Hill CT1: Cant 6H 5 (3G 43)
Oaten Hill Ct. CT1: Cant 3G 43
Oaten Hill Pl. CT1: Cant 6G 5 (3G 43)
Oaze, The CT5: Whit 1E 31
Observatory Way CT12: Ram 1A 36
    (not continuous)
Ocean Cl. CT7: Birch 5F 9
Ocean Vw. CT6: Belt 1A 20
    CT10: B'stairs 6G 29
Ocivan Way CT9: Mgte 2A 28
Odeon Cinema
    Canterbury 5G 5 (2G 43)
Offley Cl. CT9: Mgte 4C 12
Ogilvy Ct. CT10: St Pet 6E 13
Olantigh Ct. CT7: Birch 6E 9
Olave Rd. CT9: Mgte 4A 12
Old Boundary Rd. CT8: Wgte S 4B 10
Old Brewery Bus. Cen CT1: Cant 3D 4
Old Brewery Lofts ME13: Fav 3F 47
    (off Church St.)
Old Bridge Rd. CT5: Whit 4G 15
Old Coach House, The CT9: Mgte 2H 7
    (off Bath Rd.)
Old Council Yd. CT10: St Pet 6D 12
Old Crossing Rd. CT9: Mgte 4D 10
Old Dairy Cl. CT11: Ram 2D 6 (2F 37)
Old Dover Rd. CT1: Cant 6F 5 (3G 43)
Old Farm Cl. CT5: Whit 1E 31
Old Farm Rd. CT7: Birch 6B 8
Old Fold CT5: Ches .5C 16
Old Green Rd. CT9: Mgte 4C 12
    CT10: St Pet 6F 13
Old Hall Dr. CT12: C'snd 4E 35
Oldhawe Hill CT6: Broom 6G 19

Old Kingsdown Cl. CT10: B'stairs 4E 29
Old Palace, The
    Canterbury 1F 5
Old Palace Rd. CT4: Bek, Patr 6G 45
Old Park Av. CT1: Cant 6A 40
Old Park Ct. CT1: Cant 6A 40
Old Post Office, The CT1: Cant 2D 4
Old Printworks Cl. CT5: Whit 5F 15
Old Rd. CT10: B'stairs 4F 13
Old Ruttington La. CT1: Cant 1H 5 (1G 43)
Old School, The ME13: Fav 4F 47
Old School Cl. CT2: Sturry 2D 40
Old School Gdns. CT9: Mgte 6H 7 (4A 12)
Old School Row CT11: Ram 2C 36
Old School Yd. CT10: St Pet 2E 29
    (off Ranelagh Gro.)
Old Stables, The CT9: Mgte 3H 7
Old Timber Yd. Ind. Est. CT12: Ram 2H 35
Old Vicarage Gdn. CT2: Sturry 2D 40
Old Watling St. CT1: Cant 3A 4 (2F 43)
Old Weavers House, The
    Canterbury 2D 4
Olive Gro. CT11: Ram 1D 6 (1F 37)
Olympia Way CT5: Whit 5H 15
Omer Av. CT9: Clift .3C 12
Orange St. CT1: Cant 2E 5 (2F 43)
Orchard, The CT12: Monk'n 3B 32
Orchard Cl. CT2: Cant 4F 39
    CT5: Tank 2H 15
    CT12: Minst 2F 33
    CT12: Ram 4B 28
Orchard Ct. CT6: Hern 6D 18
Orchard End CT11: Ram 4A 36
Orchard Flats CT1: Cant 3B 44
Orchard Gdns. CT9: Mgte 4C 10
Orchard Gro. CT5: Whit 5F 15
    (off Gordon Rd.)
Orchard La. CT7: St N 6F 23
Orchard Pk. Homes CT6: Belt 3H 19
Orchard Pl. ME13: Fav 4F 47
Orchard Residences, The CT1: Cant 5G 43
Orchard Rd. CT6: H Bay 4D 18
    CT9: Mgte 5C 10
Orchard Row CT6: Hern 6E 19
Orchard St. CT2: Cant 1E 43
Orchard St. M. CT2: Cant 1E 43
Orchard Vs. CT2: Sturry 4D 40
Orient Pl. CT2: Cant 1F 43
Osborne Gdns. CT6: Belt 2H 19
Osborne Rd. CT10: B'stairs 3F 29
Osborne Ter. CT9: Mgte 5H 7 (4H 11)
Osbourn Av. CT8: Wgte S 5A 10
Oscar Rd. CT10: B'stairs 3H 29
Osprey Cl. CT5: Whit 6E 15
OSPRINGE 5D 46
Ospringe Pl. ME13: Fav 5D 46
Ospringe Rd. ME13: Fav 5C 46
Ospringe St. ME13: Fav, Osp 5C 46
Otham Cl. CT2: Cant 4G 39
Owl's Hatch Rd. CT6: H Bay 5H 17
Oxenden Pk. Dr. CT6: H Bay 3C 18
Oxenden Sq. CT6: H Bay 2C 18
Oxenden St. CT6: H Bay 2C 18
    (not continuous)
Oxford Cl. CT5: Whit 4F 15
Oxford Ct. CT1: Cant 3F 43
Oxford Rd. CT1: Cant 3F 43
Oxford St. CT5: Whit 4F 15
    CT9: Mgte .5G 7 (4H 11)
Oxney Cl. CT7: Birch 6D 8
Oyster Cl. CT6: H Bay 2H 17
OysterCoast Watersports 2F 15
    (off Whitstable Harbour)
Oyster Indoor Bowling Centre, The 2F 15
Oysters, The CT5: Whit 2G 15
Ozengell Pl. CT12: Ram 5A 28

P

Pacific Cl. CT5: Whit 5H 15
Packers La. CT11: Ram 3C 6 (2E 37)
Paddock, The CT1: Cant 2H 43
Paddock Rd. CT7: Birch 6E 9
Paddocks, The CT4: Bek 6H 45
    CT6: Belt 2A 20
    CT9: Mgte 4C 12
    CT10: B'stairs 6F 13
Paddock Vw. CT5: Whit 6F 15
Paffard Cl. CT2: Sturry 1D 40
Palace Cinema 3H 29
    (off Fort Rd.)
Palace Cl. CT5: Swale 3B 16
Palace St. CT1: Cant 2E 5 (1F 43)
Pal Cres. CT7: Birch .2A 26
Palmars Cross Hill CT2: R Comn 1A 42

Palm Bay Av. CT9: Clift 2C 12
Palm Bay Gdns. CT9: Clift 2C 12
Palm Ct. CT8: Wgte S 4A 10
    (off Rowena Rd.)
Palmer Cl. CT6: Hern .6F 19
Palmer Cres. CT9: Mgte 5C 12
    (not continuous)
Palmerston Av. CT10: B'stairs 4H 29
Parade CT1: Cant 3E 5 (2F 43)
Parade, The CT7: Birch 5B 8
  CT9: Mgte 2F 7 (2G 11)
  CT10: B'stairs 3H 29
Paradise CT11: Ram 3A 6 (2D 36)
Paradise Row
  CT13: S'wch 4B 48
Paragon CT11: Ram 6A 6 (4D 36)
Paragon Ct. CT9: Mgte 1H 7
Paragon Prom. CT11: Ram 6A 6 (4D 36)
Paragon St. CT11: Ram 6A 6 (4D 36)
Pardoner Ct. CT2: Cant 3C 42
Parham Cl. CT1: Cant .6H 39
Parham Rd. CT1: Cant 6H 39
Parish Cl. CT10: St Pet 1E 29
Park & Ride
  New Dover Road 6A 44
  Sturry Road 5B 40
  Wincheap 4D 42
Park Av. CT5: Tank 2G 15
  CT7: Birch 1D 24
  CT10: B'stairs 5E 29
Park Chase CT10: B'stairs 5E 29
Park Cl. CT9: Mgte 4D 12
Park Cotts. CT11: Ram 5E 29
Park Ct. CT2: Sturry .2D 40
  ME13: Fav 4G 47
Park Cres. Rd.
  CT9: Mgte 4H 7 (3A 12)
Park Farm Bungs. CT2: T Hill 2E 39
Park Farm Cl. CT2: T Hill 2E 39
Park Gate CT10: B'stairs 5F 29
Parkland Ct. CT10: B'stairs 1F 29
Park La. CT7: Birch .1E 25
  CT9: Mgte 4H 7 (3H 11)
Park Pl. CT9: Mgte 4F 7 (3G 11)
Park Rd. CT6: H Bay .3D 18
  CT7: Birch, Wdchu .6F 9
  CT9: Mgte 4H 7 (3A 12)
  CT10: B'stairs 1H 29
  CT11: Ram 2A 6 (2C 36)
  ME13: Fav 5F 47
Park Royal CT6: H Bay 4F 19
Parkside Ct. CT11: Ram 2D 36
Park Vw. CT2: Sturry 2D 40
  CT9: Mgte 3A 12
  CT11: Ram 2C 36
Park Vw. Lodge ME13: Fav 4F 47
Parkway, The CT7: Birch 6F 9
Parkwood Cl. CT10: B'stairs 5E 29
Parkwood Rd. CT2: Cant 4C 38
Parsonage Flds. CT12: Monk'n 2A 32
Parsonage Rd. CT6: H Bay 4E 19
Partridge Ct. CT6: Broom 4G 19
Partridge La. ME13: Fav 3F 47
Passage, The CT9: Mgte 1H 7
Pathway, The CT10: B'stairs 2H 29
Patricia Way CT10: B'stairs 4C 28
PATRIXBOURNE 6F 45
Pavilion Ct. CT2: Cant 1E 43
Payton Cl. CT9: Mgte 1A 28
Payton M. CT1: Cant .1H 43
Pean Ct. Rd. CT5: Whit 4F 31
Pean Hill CT5: Whit 4F 31
Pearmain Wlk. CT1: Cant 3A 44
    (off Russett Rd.)
Pearsons Cotts. CT5: Whit 3E 15
Pearson's Way CT10: St Pet 6E 13
Pear Tree Cl. CT10: B'stairs 3C 28
Peartree Rd. CT6: Broom 5F 19
Peelers Ct. CT2: Cant .1F 43
    (off Kirby's La.)
PEGWELL 4A 36
Pegwell Av. CT11: Ram 4A 36
Pegwell Bay Caravan Pk. CT11: Ram 6E 35
Pegwell Bay Country Pk. 6E 35
Pegwell Cl. CT11: Ram 4A 36
Pegwell Ct. CT11: Ram 4B 36
Pegwell Rd. CT11: Ram 4A 36
Pembroke Av. CT9: Mgte 4D 10
Pembroke Ct. CT11: Ram 2C 6
Pengelly Pl. CT2: Cant 6F 39
Pennington Cl. CT2: West 1G 41
Penshurst Cl. CT2: Cant 5G 39
Penshurst Gdns. CT9: Clift 3F 13
Penshurst Ri. ME13: Fav 3D 46
Penshurst Rd. CT11: Ram 2F 37
Percy Av. CT10: B'stairs 4F 13

Percy Rd. CT9: Clift 2A 12
  CT10: St Pet 2F 29
  CT11: Ram 1A 6 (1D 36)
Peri Ct. CT1: Cant 4E 43
Perkins Av. CT9: Mgte 5H 11
Perry's Cl. ME13: Fav 3F 47
Petchell M. CT1: Cant 6H 39
    (off Teddington Cl.)
Petrel Cl. CT6: Belt 3B 20
Pettits Row ME13: Fav 4D 46
Pettman Cl. CT6: H Bay 4D 18
Pettman Ct. CT10: St Pet 2E 29
Pettman M. CT5: Whit 3E 15
Petts Cres. CT12: Minst 4F 33
Pewter Ct. CT1: Cant 3B 44
Pfizer Monks' Wall Nature Reserve 2B 48
Philip Corby Cl. CT9: Clift 3B 12
Phillips Rd. CT7: Birch 1E 25
Picton Rd. CT11: Ram 3C 36
Pie Factory
  Margate 2F 7
    (off Broad St.)
Pier, The
  Margate 1F 7 (2G 11)
Pier App. CT10: B'stairs 3H 29
Pier Av. CT5: Tank 2A 16
  CT6: H Bay 2C 18
Pier Chine CT6: H Bay 2C 18
Pierpoint Rd. CT5: Whit 6F 15
Pierremont Av. CT10: B'stairs 3G 29
Pig All. CT11: Ram 3B 6
Pigeon La. CT6: Hern 5E 19
Pike La. CT11: Ram 2C 6
Pilckem Cl. CT1: Cant 1B 44
PILGRIMS HOSPICE IN CANTERBURY 1D 42
PILGRIMS HOSPICE IN THANET 6H 11
Pilgrims La. CT5: Seas 2D 30
Pilgrims Rd. CT1: Cant 3A 44
Pilgrims Way CT1: Cant 3H 43
  CT2: Harb 2A 42
Pinball Parlour, The
  Ramsgate 5A 6
    (off Ivy La.)
Pines, The CT1: Cant 4G 43
    (off Puckle La.)
  CT10: B'stairs 3D 28
Pine Tree Av. CT2: Cant 6E 39
Pine Tree Cl. CT7: Birch 6F 9
    (off The Parkway)
Pinetree Cl. CT5: Tank 2H 15
Pine Wlk. CT6: Belt .2A 20
Pinewood Cl. CT12: Ram 6C 28
Pin Hill CT1: Cant 6B 4 (3F 43)
Pintail Way CT6: Broom 5G 19
Pioneer Bus. Pk. CT11: Ram 1D 36
Piper Ct. CT12: Ram .6C 28
Plains of Waterloo CT11: Ram 3C 6 (2E 37)
Plantation Rd. CT5: Ches 3D 16
  ME13: Fav 4E 47
Plaxton Way CT6: H Bay 4E 19
Playhouse Theatre
  Whitstable 4F 15
Plenty Brook Dr. CT6: H Bay 4D 18
Pleydell Cres. CT2: Sturry 1D 40
Plough Ct. CT6: Broom 5G 19
Plough La. CT5: Swale 2D 16
Plover Cl. CT6: Belt 2B 20
Pluckley Gdns. CT9: Clift 3E 13
Plumpton Wlk. CT1: Cant 1H 43
Plumpudding La. ME13: Darg 6A 30
Plumstone Rd. CT7: Acol 6C 24
  CT12: Monk'n 6C 24
Plum Tree Gro. CT7: Birch 6D 8
Pochard Cres. CT6: H Bay 4C 18
Poets Cnr. CT9: Mgte 5H 7 (4H 11)
Poldark Ct. CT11: Ram 2F 37
    (off Victoria Pde.)
Pollard Pl. CT5: Whit .1E 31
PoloFarm Sports Club 1D 44
Polo Way CT5: Ches .4D 16
Pond Cotts. CT6: Broom 5H 19
Pondicherry All. CT13: S'wch 4C 48
    (off Up. Strand St.)
Poorhole La. CT10: B'stairs 2B 28
Popes La. CT2: Sturry 1C 40
Poplar Dr. CT6: H Bay 5A 18
Poplar Rd. CT10: St Pet 1E 29
  CT11: Ram 3A 6 (2D 36)
Poplar Row CT7: Birch 2A 26
Portland Cl. CT11: Ram 2C 6 (2E 37)
Portland Sq. CT1: Cant 3H 43
Portland Rd. CT9: Mgte 2F 27
Portlight Pl. CT5: Whit 1C 30
Portway CT5: Whit 5E 15
Post Ter. CT5: Whit 3G 15
POTTEN STREET 3D 22

Potten St. CT7: St N .3D 22
Potten St. Rd. CT7: St N 3D 22
Potter St. CT13: S'wch 4C 48
Poulders Gdns. CT13: S'wch 6A 48
    (not continuous)
Poulders Rd. CT13: S'wch 5A 48
Pound Ct. CT1: Cant 1B 4 (1F 43)
Powell Cotton Dr. CT7: Birch 1F 25
Powell-Cotton Mus. 2F 25
Precincts, The CT1: Cant 1F 5 (1G 43)
Prestedge Av. CT11: Ram 5E 29
PRESTON 5F 47
Preston Av. ME13: Fav 6G 47
Preston Gro. ME13: Fav 5F 47
Preston La. ME13: Fav 5F 47
    (Preston Pk.)
  ME13: Fav 5E 47
    (Preston St.)
Preston Malthouse ME13: Fav 5F 47
Preston Pde. CT5: Seas 6A 14
Preston Pk. ME13: Fav 5F 47
Preston Parks CT12: Mans 5G 27
Preston Pl. ME13: Fav . . . . .5F 4.
    (off Chapel St.)
Preston Rd. CT12: Mans 4F 27
Preston St. ME13: Fav 5E 47
    (not continuous)
Pretoria Rd. CT1: Cant 2H 43
Price's Av. CT9: Mgte 3A 12
  CT11: Ram 3C 36
Priest Av. CT2: Cant .2C 42
Priest Flds. CT6: Belt 2B 20
Priest Wlk. CT5: Tank 2B 16
Primrose Cott. Caravan Pk.
  CT5: Whit 6H 15
Primrose Way CT5: Ches 4C 16
  CT12: C'snd 4E 3
Prince Andrew Rd. CT10: St Pet 6E 1
Prince Charles Rd. CT10: St Pet 6E 13
Prince Edward's Prom. CT11: Ram 4B 3
Prince of Wales Youth Club and Sports Cen.
  . . . . .6H 3
Prince's Av. CT12: Ram 6B 2
Princes Cl. CT7: Birch .6B
Princes Cres. CT9: Mgte 4G 7 (3H 11)
Prince's Rd. CT11: Ram 1D 3
Prince's Gdns. CT9: Clift 3C 1
Princess Anne Rd. CT10: St Pet 6E 1
Princess Cl. CT5: Swale 2C 1
Princess Margaret Av. CT9: Clift 3D 1
  CT12: Ram 6A 2
    (not continuous)
Princess Rd. CT5: Tank 2C 1
Princes St. CT9: Mgte 3F 7 (3H 11)
  CT11: Ram 4B 6 (3E 37)
Prince's Wlk. CT9: Clift . . . . .2E 1.
Princes Way CT2: Cant 1D 4:
Prioress Rd. CT2: Cant 2D 4:
Priory Cl. CT10: B'stairs 4F 2
Priory Courtyard CT11: Ram 5A 6 (3D 36)
Priory Gdns. CT1: Cant 4G 4
Priory La. CT6: H Bay 4E 1
Priory M. CT11: Ram .5A
Priory of St Jacob CT1: Cant 4E 4
Priory Pl. ME13: Fav .2E 4
Priory Rd. CT11: Ram 5A 6 (3D 36)
  ME13: Fav 3D 4
Priory Row ME13: Fav 3E 4
Pritchard Cl. CT1: Cant 4G 4
Promenade CT5: Tank 2H 1
    (not continuous)
  CT7: Birch 5D
  CT9: Mgte 2G 1
Promenade, The CT9: Clift 2A 1
  CT10: B'stairs 4H 2
Prospect Cl. CT8: Wgte S 6A 1
Prospect Ct. CT11: Ram 5B
Prospect Gdns. CT12: Minst 2F 3
Prospect Hill CT6: H Bay 2E 1
Prospect Pl. CT1: Cant 3G 4
  CT7: St N 6E 2
  CT10: B'stairs 3H 2
Prospect Rd. CT7: Birch 6D
  CT10: B'stairs 3H 2
  CT12: Minst 3F 3
Prospect Ter. CT11: Ram 5B 6 (3E 37)
Provender Wlk. ME13: Fav 3F 4
Providence Row CT1: Cant 3E 4
Puckle Ho. CT1: Cant .3G 4
Puckle La. CT1: Cant .4G 4
Puffin Rd. CT6: Belt 3A 2
Pullman Ct. CT12: Ram 6C 2
Pump La. CT9: Mgte 3G 7 (3H 1
Purchas Ct. CT2: Cant 4C 3
Pye All. La. CT5: Whit 4D 3
Pyott M. CT1: Cant 2H 1

Pyson's Rd. CT10: B'stairs, Ram 5C 28
   CT12: Ram 5C 28
Pyson's Rd. Ind. Est. CT10: B'stairs 4D 28

Q

Quantock Gdns. CT12: Ram 4B 28
Quay, The CT13: S'wch 4C 48
Quay Ct. CT5: Whit 3G 15
Quay La. CT13: S'wch 4C 48
   ME13: Fav 3F 47
Queen Bertha Rd. CT11: Ram 3C 36
Queen Bertha's Av. CT7: Birch 5G 9
Queen Elizabeth Av. CT9: Mgte 4D 12
QUEEN ELIZABETH THE QUEEN MOTHER HOSPITAL
   . . . . .5H 11
Queens Arms Yd. CT9: Mgte 2F 7
   (off Market St.)
Queens Av. CT2: Cant 1D 42
   CT6: Belt 2H 19
   CT7: Birch 6B 8
   CT9: Mgte 5F 7 (4G 11)
   CT10: B'stairs 1H 29
   CT12: Ram 6B 28
Queensbridge Dr. CT6: H Bay 2A 18
Queens Ct. CT6: H Bay 3E 19
   CT9: Clift 2A 12
   CT11: Ram 4B 6
QUEENSDOWN 4B 26
Queensdown Rd. CT7: Wdchu 3B 26
Queens Gdns. CT6: H Bay 2D 18
   CT9: Clift 2A 12
   CT10: B'stairs 4H 29
Queen's Ga. Rd. CT11: Ram 1C 36
Queens Pde. CT9: Clift 2A 12
   ME13: Fav 4F 47
   (off East St.)
Queens Rd. CT5: Tank 3H 15
   CT8: Wgte S 5B 10
   CT10: B'stairs 3G 29
   CT11: Ram 2F 37
   ME13: Fav 4D 46
Queen St. CT6: H Bay 2D 18
   CT9: Mgte 3F 7 (3G 11)
   CT11: Ram 4B 6 (3D 36)
QUEEN VICTORIA MEMORIAL HOSPITAL 3F 19
Quenin Gate (remains of)
   Canterbury 2H 5
Querns Pl. CT1: Cant 2H 43
Querns Rd. CT1: Cant 2A 44
Quetta Rd. CT12: Ram 6H 27
Quex Caravan Pk. CT7: Birch 2H 25
Quex Ct. CT7: Birch 1F 25
   (off Powell Cotton Dr.)
Quex House & Gardens 2F 25
Quex Pk. 2G 25
Quex Rd. CT8: Wgte S 5B 10
Quex Vw. Rd. CT7: Birch 1D 24
Quinneys Pl. CT5: Swale 3C 16

R

Radley Cl. CT10: B'stairs 1G 29
Radnor Cl. CT6: Broom 6F 19
Radnor M. CT1: Cant 6H 39
RAF Manston History Mus. 5C 26
RAF Manston Spitfire & Hurricane Memorial Mus.
   . . . . .5C 26
Raglan Pl. CT10: B'stairs 3H 29
Railway Av. CT5: Whit 4G 15
Railway Cotts. CT5: Whit 3G 15
   (off Station Rd.)
Railway Ter. CT9: Mgte 4F 11
Raleigh Cl. CT11: Ram 1D 6
Ramsey Cl. CT2: Cant 1E 43
Ramsey Ho. CT1: Cant 3F 43
   (off Pin Hill)
RAMSGATE 3B 6 (2E 37)
Ramsgate Maritime Mus. 5C 6 (3F 37)
Ramsgate Rd. CT9: B'stairs, Mgte 6G 7 (4H 11)
   CT10: B'stairs, Ram 4F 29
   CT11: B'stairs 6F 29
   CT13: S'wch 4F 29
Ramsgate Sports Cen. 3A 6 (2D 36)
Ramsgate Station (Rail) 1C 36
Ramsgate Swimming Pool 1C 36
Rancorn Rd. CT9: Mgte 4E 11
Randolph Cl. CT1: Cant 4G 43
Randolph Sq. CT9: Mgte 2H 7 (2H 11)
Ranelagh Gdns. CT10: St Pet 2E 29
Ranelagh Gro. CT10: St Pet 2E 29
Ransome Way CT7: Birch 1E 25
Ravensbourne Av. CT6: Hern 4F 19
Ravenscourt Rd. CT2: R Comn 5B 38

Rawdon Rd. CT11: Ram 3B 36
Rayham Rd. CT5: Whit 5A 16
Raymond Av. CT1: Cant 4G 43
READING STREET 6F 13
Reading St. CT10: B'stairs 5F 13
Reading St. Rd. CT10: B'stairs 4E 13
Rebecca Ct. CT9: Mgte 3B 12
Rectory Ct. CT5: Swale 3D 16
Rectory Gdns. CT5: Swale 3D 16
Rectory Rd. CT10: B'stairs 2H 29
RECULVER 1F 21
Reculver Av. CT7: Birch 5C 8
Reculver Ct. CT6: Belt 1B 20
Reculver Country Pk. 1D 20
Reculver Dr. CT6: Belt 2A 20
Reculver La. CT6: Rec 2C 20
Reculver Rd. CT6: Belt 4G 19
Reculvers Rd. CT8: Wgte S 6B 10
Redcot La. CT7: Sturry 1F 41
Redgates CT6: H Bay 2E 19
Redhill Rd. CT8: Wgte S 5A 10
Red Lion La. CT5: Whit 3F 15
Redwood Cl. CT2: Cant 6E 39
Reed Av. CT1: Cant 6A 40
Reedland Cres. ME13: Fav 3E 47
Reeds Cl. CT6: H Bay 3F 19
Reeves All. CT5: Whit 4F 15
   (off Middle Wall)
Reeves Cl. CT2: Cant 2C 42
Reeves Way CT5: Ches 4C 16
Reeves Yd. CT5: Whit 3F 15
Regency Cl. CT5: Whit 6G 15
Regency Pl. CT1: Cant 6H 39
Regent Dr. CT6: H Bay 4F 19
Regent St. CT5: Whit 3F 15
Regents Wlk. CT6: Belt 2H 19
Reliance Dr. CT6: H Bay 4F 19
Remston M. CT1: Cant 6H 39
Renault Cl. CT6: H Bay 1G 17
Rendezvous, The CT9: Mgte 2F 7 (2G 11)
Repton Cl. CT10: St Pet 1F 29
Reservoir Rd. CT5: Whit 3G 15
Retreat, The CT7: Birch 5F 9
   CT12: Ram 1B 36
Revolution Climbing Cen. 6D 12
Reynolds Cl. CT3: H Bay 3F 19
Reynolds Farm Rd. CT3: H Bay, Hoath 5E 21
Reynolds La. CT3: M'sde 4F 21
Rheims Ct. CT2: Cant 1D 42
Rheims Way CT1: Cant 4A 4 (2E 43)
   CT2: Cant 3A 4 (1D 42)
Rhodaus Cl. CT1: Cant 3F 43
Rhodaus Town CT1: Cant 6D 4 (3F 43)
Rhodes Gdns. CT10: B'stairs 1G 29
Richard Ct. CT9: Mgte 3B 12
Richardson Way CT12: C'snd 3E 35
Richborough Bus. Pk. CT13: S'wch 2B 48
Richborough Rd. CT8: Wgte S 6B 10
   CT13: S'wch 1A 48
Richborough Roman Fort & Amphitheatre 1A 48
Richborough Way CT12: C'snd, Ram 6C 34
Richmond Av. CT9: Mgte 4B 12
Richmond Ct. CT6: H Bay 2C 18
Richmond Dr. CT6: Belt 3A 20
Richmond Gdns. CT2: Cant 6C 38
Richmond Rd. CT5: Whit 4B 16
   CT11: Ram 4A 6 (3D 36)
Richmond St. CT6: H Bay 2D 18
Ridgeway CT5: Ches, Whit 4B 16
Ridgeway, The CT9: Mgte 4B 12
   CT10: B'stairs 4F 29
Ridgeway Cliff CT6: H Bay 2A 18
Riding Ga. Pl. CT1: Cant 5E 5
Ridings, The CT1: Cant 1H 43
   CT5: Ches 4D 16
   CT9: Clift 2E 13
Ridley Cl. CT6: Hern 6E 19
Rigby Ct. CT1: Cant 6H 39
Riley Av. CT6: H Bay 1F 17
Ringould Av. CT12: Ram 1A 36
Ringsloe Ct. CT7: Birch 5B 8
   (off The Parade)
Ringwood Cl. CT2: Cant 5E 39
Ripple Cl. CT1: Cant 6A 40
Risdon Cl. CT2: Sturry 2D 40
River Bend Ct. CT2: Cant 6G 39
Riverdale Rd. CT11: Ram 6H 39
Riverhead Dr. CT9: Mgte 6G 39
Rivers Ct. CT12: Minst 4G 33
Riversdale Rd. CT12: Ram 6A 28
Riverside Ct. CT2: Cant 1F 43
Riverside Ind. Est. CT1: Cant 5H 39
Riverside Retail Pk. CT1: Cant 3D 42
River Vw. CT2: Sturry 1D 40

Roberts Rd. CT5: Seas 1B 30
Rochester Av. CT1: Cant 4H 43
Rochester Ct. CT1: Cant 4H 43
Rockingham Pl. CT6: Broom 5F 19
Rockstone Way CT12: Ram 6A 28
Rodney St. CT11: Ram 5A 6 (3D 36)
Roebuck Rd. ME13: Fav 4C 46
   ME13: Fav 4E 47
Roman Rd. CT12: Ram 5B 28
Romilly Gdns. CT12: Ram 5C 28
Romney Cl. CT7: Birch 6E 9
Romney Gdns. CT12: Ram 5C 28
Roper Cl. CT2: Cant 1E 43
Roper Rd. CT2: Cant 1E 43
Rope Walk, The CT1: Cant 5A 4 (2E 43)
   CT13: S'wch 5B 48
Rope Wlk. Ho. CT9: Mgte 4F 7
   (off High St.)
Rope Wlk. M. CT13: S'wch 4B 48
Roseacre Cl. CT2: Cant 1E 43
Roseacre Ct. CT9: Clift 5D 10
Rosebery Av. CT6: Belt 2A 20
   CT11: Ram 6F 29
Rose Cott. CT6: Broom 4H 19
Rosedale Rd. CT9: Mgte 4A 12
Rose Gdns. CT6: H Bay 3G 19
   CT7: Birch 1D 24
   CT12: Minst 3F 33
Rose Hill CT11: Ram 4B 6 (3E 37)
Roselands Gdns. CT2: Cant 6D 38
Rose La. CT1: Cant 5E 5 (2F 43)
Roselawn Gdns. CT9: Garl 5D 10
Roselea Av. CT6: H Bay 4D 18
Rosemary Av. CT10: B'stairs 5F 29
Rosemary Gdns. CT5: Whit 5A 16
   CT10: B'stairs 5F 29
Rosemary La. CT1: Cant 5B 4 (2F 43)
Rose Ter. ME13: Fav 6F 47
Rosetower Ct. CT10: B'stairs 5F 13
Rosewood Way CT7: Birch 6F 9
Rosiers Ct. CT2: Cant 1E 43
Rossetti Rd. CT7: Birch 5D 8
Ross Gdns. CT2: R Comn 5A 38
Rossland Rd. CT12: Ram 1A 36
Rothsay Ct. CT11: Ram 6F 29
ROUGH COMMON 5B 38
Rough Comn. Rd. CT2: R Comn 6A 38
Rowan Cl. CT2: Sturry 2D 40
Rowan Ct. CT10: St Pet 2G 29
Rowan Tree Pk. CT5: Seas 1C 30
Rowe Cl. CT9: Mgte 6H 11
Rowena Rd. CT8: Wgte S 4A 10
Rowland Cres. CT6: Belt 2A 20
Rowland Dr. CT6: H Bay 5A 18
Roxburgh Rd. CT8: Wgte S 4B 10
Royal Av. CT5: Whit 2E 31
Royal Cinema, The
   Faversham 4F 47
Royal Cl. CT10: B'stairs 3F 29
Royal Cres. CT9: Mgte 3F 11
   CT11: Ram 6A 6 (4D 36)
Royal Esplanade CT9: Mgte 4B 36
Royal Harbour App. CT11: Ram 3A 36
   (not continuous)
Royal M. CT11: Ram 2D 6
Royal Native Way CT5: Whit 1C 30
Royal Oak Camping and Caravan
   CT2: B Oak 1B 40
Royal Pde. CT11: Ram 5B 6 (3E 37)
Royal Rd. CT11: Ram 5A 6 (3D 36)
Royal Sands CT11: Ram 4D 6 (3F 37)
Royal Seabathing, The CT9: Mgte 3E 11
Royal Temple Yacht Club
   Ramsgate 4B 6
   (off Westcliff Arc.)
Rugby Cl. CT10: St Pet 2F 29
Rumfields Rd. CT10: B'stairs 3C 28
Runcie Ho. CT1: Cant 3F 43
   (off Station Rd.)
Runcie Pl. CT2: Cant 1D 42
Runnymede M. ME13: Fav 4E 47
Rushmead Ct. CT2: Cant 6D 38
Ruskins Vw. CT6: Hern 6E 19
Russell Dr. CT5: Swale 2D 16
Russell Pl. ME13: Oare 1D 46
Russet Av. ME13: Fav 6G 47
Russets, The CT5: Ches 4D 16
Russett Rd. CT1: Cant 3A 44
Rutherford College CT2: Cant 4E 39
Rutland Av. CT9: Clift 3B 12
Rutland Cl. CT1: Cant 3B 44
Rutland Gdns. CT7: Birch 6D 8
   CT9: Clift 3C 12
Rydal Av. CT11: Ram 2A 36
Ryder Cl. CT6: Hern 5E 19
Ryder's Av. CT8: Wgte S 5H 9

Ryde St.—Scott Av.

Ryde St. CT2: Cant 1E 43
Rye Wlk. CT6: Broom 5G 19

S

Sackett's Gap CT9: Clift 2C 12
Sacketts Hill CT10: B'stairs 1B 28
Saddlers M. CT5: Ches 4D 16
CT12: Ram 6H 27
Saddleton Gro. CT5: Whit 5F 15
Saddleton Rd. CT5: Whit 5F 15
Sail Lofts, The CT5: Whit 3F 15
St Alphege Cl. CT5: Whit 6D 14
St Alphege La. CT1: Cant 1E 5 (1F 43)
St Andrews Cl. CT1: Cant 6A 4 (3E 43)
CT5: Whit 6G 15
CT6: H Bay 3E 19
CT9: Mgte 6H 11
St Andrews Ho. CT1: Cant 6B 4
St Andrews Lees CT13: S'wch 5C 48
St Andrew's Rd. CT11: Ram 1F 37
St Anne's Ct. CT6: H Bay 2C 18
St Anne's Dr. CT6: H Bay 3B 18
St Anne's Gdns. CT9: Mgte 5H 11
St Anne's Rd. CT5: Tank 2H 15
St Ann's Rd. ME13: Fav 4D 46
St Anthony's Way CT9: Mgte 4C 12
St Augustine's Abbey
Canterbury 4H 5 (2G 43)
Ramsgate 6A 6 (4D 36)
St Augustine's Abbey Mus. 2G 43
St Augustine's Av. CT9: Mgte 5H 11
St Augustines Bus. Pk. CT5: Swale 3E 17
St Augustines Ct. CT1: Cant 1H 43
CT6: H Bay 4D 18
St Augustine's Cres. CT5: Swale 2D 16
St Augustine's Cross 4E 35
St Augustines Golf Course 4D 34
St Augustines Pk. CT8: Wgte S 5A 10
CT11: Ram 3C 36
St Augustine's Rd. CT1: Cant 3H 43
CT11: Ram 6A 6 (4D 36)
St Bartholomews CT13: S'wch 5C 48
St Bart's Rd. CT13: S'wch 5A 48
St Benedict's Lawn CT11: Ram 6A 6 (4D 36)
St Benet's Rd. CT8: Wgte S 6A 10
St Bennetts *CT11: Ram 6A 6*
(off Paragon St.)
St Catherines Ct. CT11: Ram 6E 29
St Catherine's Dr. ME13: Fav 5F 47
St Catherine's Gro. CT12: Mans 6F 27
St Christopher Cl. CT9: Mgte 5D 12
St Christopher's Grn. CT10: St Pet 2F 29
St Christophers M. CT11: Ram 1D 36
St Clements CT13: S'wch 5C 48
St Clements Ct. CT6: H Bay 4E 19
CT10: St Pet 2E 29
CT11: Ram 2A 6 (2D 36)
St Clements Rd. CT8: Wgte S 4A 10
St Crispin's Rd. CT8: Wgte S 6A 10
St David's Cl. CT5: Whit 5G 15
CT7: Birch 5F 9
St David's Rd. CT11: Ram 6F 29
ST DUNSTAN'S 1D 42
St Dunstans Cl. CT2: Cant 1E 43
St Dunstans Ct. CT2: Cant 1E 43
St Dunstan's Rd. CT9: Mgte 3A 12
St Dunstan's St. CT2: Cant 1B 4 (1E 43)
St Dunstan's Ter. CT2: Cant 1E 43
St Edmunds Rd. CT1: Cant 4B 4 (2F 43)
St Francis Cl. CT5: Whit 6G 15
CT9: Mgte 5D 12
St George's Av. CT6: H Bay 3A 18
St George's Cen. CT1: Cant 5H 5 (2G 43)
St Georges Cl. CT5: Whit 6G 15
St Georges Hall of Residence CT1: Cant 5G 5
St George's La. CT1: Cant 5E 5 (2F 43)
St George's Lees CT13: S'wch 5C 48
(not continuous)
St Georges Pl. CT1: Cant 5G 5 (2G 43)
CT13: S'wch 5D 48
St George's Rd. CT10: B'stairs 3G 29
CT11: Ram 1D 6 (1F 37)
CT13: S'wch 5C 48
St George's St. CT1: Cant 4F 5 (2G 43)
St George's Ter. CT1: Cant 6E 5
CT6: H Bay 2B 18
St George's Tower
Canterbury 4F 5
St Gregory's Ct. CT1: Cant 1H 43
St Gregory's Rd. CT1: Cant 1H 43
St Jacob's Pl. CT1: Cant 4D 42
St James Av. CT10: St Pet 2E 29
CT12: Ram 5B 28
St James Gdns. CT5: Whit 5F 15
St James Pk. Rd. CT9: Mgte 5C 10
St James's Ter. CT7: Birch 5F 9
St James Ter. CT7: Birch 5F 9
St Jean's Rd. CT8: Wgte S 6A 10
St John's Almshouses *CT1: Cant 1G 43*
(off St John's Pl.)
St John's Av. CT12: Ram 6H 27
St Johns Cres. CT2: T Hill 1D 38
St John's Hospital CT1: Cant 1G 43
St John's La. CT1: Cant 5C 4 (2F 43)
St Johns Pl. CT1: Cant 1G 43
CT5: Swale 2D 16
St John's Rd. CT5: Swale 3D 16
CT9: Mgte 4G 7 (3H 11)
ME13: Fav 5F 47
St John's St. CT9: Mgte 4G 7 (3H 11)
St Julien Av. CT1: Cant 1B 44
ST LAWRENCE 2C 36
St Lawrence Av. CT11: Ram 3B 36
St Lawrence Chase CT11: Ram 2B 36
St Lawrence Cl. CT1: Cant 4H 43
St Lawrence Ct. CT1: Cant 4H 43
CT11: Ram 2B 36
St Lawrence Forstal CT1: Cant 4H 43
St Lawrence Ground 4H 43
St Lawrence Ind. Est. CT11: Ram 1B 36
St Lawrence Rd. CT1: Cant 4H 43
St Louis Gro. CT6: H Bay 3A 18
St Luke's Av. CT11: Ram 1A 6 (1D 36)
St Lukes Cl. CT5: Whit 6G 15
CT8: Wgte S 5A 10
St Lukes Ct. CT11: Ram 2C 6
St Luke's Rd. CT11: Ram 1C 6 (1E 37)
St Magnus Cl. CT7: Birch 5D 8
St Magnus Ct. CT7: Birch 5E 9
St Margarets Cl. CT5: Seas 1C 30
St Margarets Rd. CT7: Wdchu 4B 26
CT8: Wgte S 6A 10
St Margaret's St. CT1: Cant 4D 4 (2F 43)
St Mark's Cl. CT5: Whit 5G 15
ST MARTIN'S 2H 43
St Martin's Av. CT1: Cant 2H 43
St Martin's Cl. CT1: Cant 2H 43
St Martins Ct. CT1: Cant 2H 43
St Martin's Hill CT1: Cant 2A 44
ST MARTIN'S HOSPITAL 2B 44
St Martin's Pl. CT1: Cant 2H 43
St Martin's Rd. CT1: Cant 2H 43
St Martin's Ter. CT1: Cant 2H 43
St Martin's Vw. CT6: Hern 6E 19
St Mary Magdalene's Tower
Canterbury 3G 5
St Mary's Av. CT9: Mgte 4D 12
St Mary's Ct. CT1: Cant 5A 4 (2E 43)
CT6: H Bay 3C 18
St Mary's Ga. CT13: S'wch 4C 48
St Mary's Gro. CT5: Seas 1A 30
St Mary's Rd. CT10: B'stairs 3H 29
CT12: Minst 3F 33
ME13: Fav 5F 47
St Mary's St. CT1: Cant 5C 4 (2F 43)
St Michaels All. CT11: Ram 4B 6 (3E 37)
St Michael's Av. CT9: Mgte 5D 12
St Michaels Cl. CT2: R Comn 1A 42
St Michael's Pl. CT2: Cant 6E 39
St Michael's Rd. CT2: Cant 5E 39
(not continuous)
St Mildred's Av. CT7: Birch 6C 8
CT10: B'stairs 3G 29
CT11: Ram 3C 36
St Mildreds Ct. CT1: Cant 3A 4 (2E 43)
CT8: Wgte S 4B 10
(off Beach Rd.)
St Mildred's Gdns. CT8: Wgte S 4B 10
St Mildred's Pl. CT1: Cant 3E 43
St Mildred's Rd. CT8: Wgte S 4A 10
CT9: Mgte 3A 12
CT11: Ram 3C 36
CT12: Minst 4F 33
St Mildreds Wlk. *CT8: Wgte S 4A 10*
(off Ethelbert Sq.)
ST NICHOLAS AT WADE 5F 23
St Nicholas Camping Site CT7: St N 5E 23
St Nicholas Cl. CT2: Sturry 1D 40
St Nicholas Ct. CT7: St N 4D 22
St Nicholas Hospital CT2: Harb 1B 42
St Nicholas Rd. CT1: Cant 4C 42
ME13: Fav 4C 46
St Patricks Cl. CT5: Whit 6G 15
St Patrick's Rd. CT11: Ram 1F 37
St Paul's Av. ME13: Fav 4C 46
St Paul's M. *CT9: Clift 2A 12*
(off St Paul's Rd.)
St Paul's Rd. CT9: Clift 2A 12
St Paul's Ter. CT1: Cant 4H 5 (2G 43)
ST PETER'S 2E 29
St Peter's Ct. CT1: Cant 1C 4
CT10: St Pet 1F 29
ME13: Fav 4C 46
St Peter's Footpath CT9: Mgte 5H 7 (4H 11)
CT10: St Pet 5A 12
St Peter's Gro. CT1: Cant 3B 4 (2F 43)
St Peter's La. CT1: Cant 1C 4 (1F 43)
St Peter's Pk. Rd. CT10: St Pet 2F 29
St Peter's Pl. CT1: Cant 3A 4 (2E 43)
St Peter's Rd. CT5: Whit 3F 15
CT9: Mgte 5G 7 (4H 11)
(not continuous)
CT10: B'stairs, St Pet 2E 29
St Peters St. CT1: Cant 1C 4 (1F 43)
CT13: S'wch 4C 48
St Radigunds Pl. CT1: Cant 1G 43
St Radigund's St. CT1: Cant 1F 43
St Saviour's Cl. ME13: Fav 4G 47
ST STEPHEN'S 6F 39
St Stephen's Cl. CT2: Cant 6F 39
St Stephen's Ct. CT2: Cant 6F 39
St Stephen's Flds. CT2: Cant 1F 43
St Stephen's Grn. CT2: Cant 5F 39
St Stephen's Hill CT2: Cant 3E 39
St Stephen's Pathway CT2: Cant 6F 39
St Stephen's Rd. CT2: Cant 5F 39
St Stephen's Trad. Est. CT2: Cant 6F 39
St Swithin's Rd. CT5: Tank 3B 16
St Thomas' Hill CT2: Cant 5C 38
St Thomas's Hospital CT13: S'wch 4B 48
St Vincents Cl. CT5: Whit 6G 15
Salisbury Av. CT10: B'stairs 4F 29
CT11: Ram 1D 6 (1F 37)
Salisbury Rd. CT2: Cant 6E 39
CT5: Whit 5F 15
CT6: H Bay 2F 19
Salmestone Ri. CT9: Mgte 5G 11
Salmestone Rd. CT9: Mgte 5G 11
Salters La. ME13: Fav 6F 47
Saltings, The *CT5: Whit 3F 15*
(off Island Wall)
Saltmarsh La. CT5: Whit 4F 15
Salts Cl. CT5: Whit 4F 15
Salts Dr. CT10: St Pet 2E 29
Saltwood Gdns. CT9: Clift 3E 13
Samuel Ct. CT9: Mgte 1H 7
Sancroft Av. CT2: Cant 1C 42
Sanctuary Cl. CT10: B'stairs 5F 29
Sandalwood Dr. CT7: St N 6F 23
Sandbanks La. ME13: G'ney 1H 47
Sand End CT5: Whit 1E 31
Sanderling Rd. CT6: Belt 3B 20
Sandhurst Cl. CT2: Cant 4G 39
Sandhurst Rd. CT9: Clift 3F 13
Sandle's Rd. CT7: Birch 6D 8
Sandown Dr. CT6: H Bay 3B 18
Sandown Lees CT13: S'wch 5C 48
Sandown Rd. CT13: S'wch 4C 48
Sandpiper Ct. *CT7: Birch 5D 8*
(off Shakespeare Rd.)
CT9: Mgte 2F 7
Sandpiper Rd. CT5: Whit 1D 30
SANDWICH 4C 48
Sandwich & Pegwell Bay National Nature Reserve
6E 35
Sandwich By-Pass CT13: S'wch 3A 48 & 5A 48
Sandwich Ind. Est. CT13: S'wch 4D 48
Sandwich Leisure Pk. CT13: S'wch 4A 48
Sandwich Rd. CT12: C'snd, Ram 6D 34
CT13: Wdboro 6A 48
Sandwich Sailing & Motor Boat Club 3D 48
Sandwich Sports & Leisure Cen. 6B 48
Sandwich Station (Rail) 5C 48
Sandwood Rd. CT11: Ram 6F 29
CT13: S'wch 5B 48
Sanger Cl. CT9: Mgte 6E 7 (4G 11)
Sangro Pl. CT1: Cant 1B 44
Sarah Gdns. CT9: Mgte 5D 12
Saras Ct. CT5: Whit 5E 15
Sarre Pl. CT13: S'wch 5B 48
Savernake Dr. CT6: Broom 5F 19
Saxon Rd. CT8: Wgte S 4B 10
CT11: Ram 3B 36
ME13: Fav 4E 47
Saxon Shore CT5: Whit 5E 15
Sceales Dr. CT12: C'snd 3F 35
Sceptre Way CT5: Whit 6D 14
School Close, The CT8: Wgte S 4A 10
School La. CT2: Blean 1A 38
CT2: Ford 4E 41
CT4: Bek 6G 45
CT6: Hern 6E 19
CT11: Ram 3B 6 (2E 37)
School Rd. CT13: S'wch 4B 48
ME13: Fav 5D 46
Scott Av. CT1: Cant 4D 42

64 A-Z Canterbury

Screaming All. CT11: Ram 6A **6** (4D **36**)
Sea App. CT10: B'stairs 3H 29
Sea Cl. CT9: Mgte 1H 7
Seacroft Rd. CT10: B'stairs 6G 29
Seafield Rd. CT5: Tank 2B 16
    CT10: B'stairs 3F 29
    CT11: Ram .2C 36
Seager Rd. ME13: Fav 2D 46
Seamark Cl. CT12: Monk'n 3B 32
Seamark Rd. CT7: Bro E, Monk'n 1B 32
Seapoint Rd. CT10: B'stairs 4H 29
Sea Rd. CT8: Wgte S 5F **9**
SEASALTER 6C 14
Seasalter Beach CT5: Whit 6C 14
Seasalter La. CT5: Seas 1C 30
Seasalter Level (Local Nature Reserve) . .2A 30
Seaside Caravan Pk. CT6: H Bay 1G 17
Sea St. CT5: Whit 3F 15
    CT6: H Bay .2H 17
Sea Vw. Av. CT7: Birch 5C **8**
Seaview Av. CT10: B'stairs 4H 29
    (off W. Cliff Rd.)
Sea Vw. Hgts. CT7: Birch 5B **8**
    (off Ethelbert Rd.)
Seaview Holiday Pk. CT5: Swale 1E 17
Sea Vw. Rd. CT6: Belt 2G 19
    CT7: Birch 5C **8**
    CT10: B'stairs 1G 29
    CT12: C'snd .3F 35
Sea Vw. Sq. CT6: H Bay 2D 18
Sea Vw. Ter. CT9: Mgte 3E 11
Seaville Dr. CT6: Belt 2A 20
Sea Wall CT5: Whit 3F 15
Seaway Cotts. CT5: Whit 4E 15
Second Av. CT9: Clift 2B 12
    CT10: B'stairs 3G 13
Secret Gdns. of Sandwich, The 4C 48
Seeshill Cl. CT5: Whit 5G 15
Selbey Cl. CT6: Belt 3G 19
Selborne Rd. CT9: Mgte 4B 12
Selling Rd. ME13: Fav 6G 47
Selsea Av. CT6: H Bay 2B 18
Selwyn Ct. CT10: St Pet 2F 29
Selwyn Dr. CT10: St Pet 2F 29
Semaphore Rd. CT7: Birch 5D **8**
Semple Cl. CT12: Minst 2G 33
Senlac Cl. CT11: Ram 3B 36
Serene Cl. CT10: B'stairs 3H 29
Serene Pl. CT10: B'stairs 3H **29**
    (off Raglan Pl.)
Setterfield Rd. CT9: Mgte 6G **7** (4H 11)
Sevastopol Pl. CT1: Cant 1B 44
Sevenacre Rd. ME13: Fav 3E 47
Seven Post All. CT13: S'wch 4C 48
    (off High St.)
SEVENSCORE 4C 34
Sevenscore Rdbt. CT12: C'snd 3D 34
Seven Stones Dr. CT10: B'stairs 6G 29
Sewell Cl. CT7: Birch 1E 25
Seymour Av. CT5: Whit 4G 15
    CT9: Mgte 4B 10
Seymour Cl. CT6: Hern 6F 19
Seymour Pl. CT1: Cant 3E 43
Shaftesbury Rd. CT2: Cant 5E 39
    CT5: Whit 4F 15
Shaftesbury St. CT11: Ram 3D **6** (2F 37)
Shah Pl. CT11: Ram 2A **6** (1D 36)
Shakespeare Pas. CT9: Mgte 3F 11
Shakespeare Rd. CT7: Birch 5D **8**
    CT9: Mgte 5G **7** (4H 11)
Shalloak Rd. CT2: B Oak 3B 40
Shallows Rd. CT10: St Pet 1C 28
Shamrock Av. CT5: Whit 6D 14
Shapland Cl. CT6: Belt 4G 19
Share & Coulter Rd. CT5: Ches 4D 16
Shearwater Av. CT5: Whit 6E 15
Sheen Ct. CT9: Mgte 4F **7** (3G 11)
Sheerways ME13: Fav 4C 46
Shelley Av. CT1: Cant 6A 44
Shell Grotto, The
    Margate 3H **7** (3H 11)
Shepherd Neame Brewery 4F 47
Shepherdsgate CT2: Cant 1F 43
Shepherds Wlk. CT5: Ches 5C 16
Shepherds Way CT5: Ches 5C 16
Sheppey Cl. CT7: Birch 6E **9**
Sheppey Vw. CT5: Whit 1E 31
Sheriffs Ct. La. CT12: Minst 4C 32
Sherwood Cl. CT5: Whit 1E 31
    CT6: Broom .5G 19
    ME13: Fav 2D 46
Sherwood Ct. CT8: Wgte S 4A 10
Sherwood Dr. CT5: Whit 1E 31
Sherwood Gdns. CT11: Ram 6E 29
Sherwood Rd. CT7: Birch 2D 24
Shipman Av. CT2: Cant 2C 42

Shipyard, The ME13: Fav 2F 47
Shirley Av. CT11: Ram 5E 29
Shore Cl. CT6: H Bay 2H 17
    CT7: Birch 5B **8**
    (off Ethelbert Rd.)
Short St. CT13: S'wch 4C 48
Shottendane Rd. CT7: Birch 3G 25
    CT9: Birch, Mgte 3G 25
Shrub Hill Rd. CT5: Ches 6D 16
Shuart La. CT7: St N 5F 23
    (not continuous)
Shunters Cl. ME13: Fav 5G 47
Shutler Rd. CT10: B'stairs 2H 29
Sidings, The CT5: Whit 3G 15
Sidings Cl. ME13: Fav 5G 47
Sidney Cooper Cl. CT2: R Comn 6B 38
Sidney Cooper Gallery 1F 43
    (off St Peter's St.)
Silvanus Ho. CT11: Ram 2A **6**
Silver Av. CT7: Birch 1F 25
Silverdale Dr. CT6: Broom 5H 19
Silverdale Rd. CT10: B'stairs 4A 36
Silvers, The CT10: B'stairs 3C 28
Simmonds Rd. CT1: Cant 3E 43
Simon Av. CT9: Clift 3D 12
Singer Av. CT6: H Bay 1H 17
Singleton Cl. CT12: Minst 3F 33
Sion Cl. CT11: Ram 5B **6**
Sion Hill CT11: Ram 5B **6** (3E **37**)
Sion Pas. CT11: Ram 5B **6**
Sir John Boy's House 1F 5
Skinners All. CT5: Whit 4F **15**
    (off King Edward St.)
Slades Cl. CT5: Ches 5C 16
Sleigh Rd. CT2: Sturry 2D 40
Sloe La. CT9: B'stairs 2B 28
Smacks All. ME13: Fav 3F 47
Smith's Hospital Almshouses CT1: Cant . .2H 43
Smugglers Leap CT12: Minst 1F 33
Smugglers Way CT7: Birch 5E **9**
Snake Drove CT3: M'sde 5F 21
Snappys Adventure Play
    South Street 6A 16
Snell Gdns. CT6: H Bay 3H 17
Sobraon Way CT1: Cant 1B 44
Solomons La. ME13: Fav 4F 47
Somerset Cl. CT5: Whit 6D 14
Somerset Cl. CT10: B'stairs 3F 29
    CT12: Ram 5B **28**
    (off Melbourne Av.)
Somerset Rd. CT1: Cant 2B 44
Somme Cl. CT1: Cant 1B 44
Sommerville Cl. ME13: Fav 4G 47
Somner Cl. CT2: Cant 1D 42
Sondes Cl. CT6: Hern 5E 19
Southall Cl. CT12: Minst 2G 33
Sth. Canterbury Rd. CT1: Cant 4G 43
Sth. Cliff Pde. CT10: B'stairs 5H 29
South Cl. CT1: Cant 3F **5** (2G **43**)
Sth. Eastern Rd. CT11: Ram 2A **6** (3C **36**)
South Lodge CT5: Tank 2G 15
Sth. Lodge Cl. CT5: Tank 2G 15
Southover Ct. CT11: Ram 3D **6**
South Rd. CT6: H Bay 3E 19
    ME13: Fav 4E 47
Southsea Dr. CT6: H Bay 3B 18
SOUTH STREET 5A 16
South St. CT1: Cant 5A 40
    CT5: Whit 5A 16
SOUTH TANKERTON 4A 16
South Vw. CT5: Whit 1F 31
Southwold Pl. CT8: Wgte S 6A 10
Southwood Gdns. CT11: Ram 2B 36
Southwood Hgts. CT11: Ram 3C 36
Southwood Rd. CT5: Tank 3B 16
    CT11: Ram 2C 36
Sowell St. CT10: St Pet 2F 29
Spa Esplanade CT6: H Bay 2A 18
Sparrow Castle CT9: Mgte 5G **7** (4H 11)
Speakman Cl. CT11: Ram 3C **36**
    (off Napleton Rd.)
Speedwell Rd. CT5: Whit 1D 30
Speke Rd. CT10: St Pet 1E 29
Speldhurst Gdns. CT9: Clift 2F 13
Spellers Ct. CT9: Mgte 2F 7
Spencer Rd. CT7: Birch 5D **8**
Spencer Sq. CT11: Ram 5A **6** (3D **36**)
Spencer St. CT11: Ram 5A **6** (3D **36**)
Spencer Wlk. CT11: Ram 5A **6**
Spenser Rd. CT6: H Bay 3C 18
Spicers Fld. CT6: Broom 5H 19
Spillett Cl. ME13: Fav 4D 46
Spinney, The CT9: Clift 4E 13
Spire Av. CT5: Whit 5H 15
Spires, The CT2: Cant 6F 39
Spitfire Way CT12: Mans 6G 25

Spratling La. CT12: Ram 6H 27
Spratling St. CT12: Mans, Ram 6F 27
Springfield Cl. CT11: Ram 5E 29
Springfield Cotts. CT4: Bek 4E 45
Springfield Rd. CT9: Clift 2E 13
Spring Gdns. CT1: Cant 3E 43
Springhead Rd. ME13: Fav 2E 47
Spring La. CT1: Cant 2H 43
    CT2: Ford 4E 41
Spring Wlk. CT5: Whit 6E 15
Square, The CT7: Birch 6E **9**
Squeeze Gut All. CT5: Whit 3F **15**
    (off Middle Wall)
Squire Av. CT2: Cant 2C 42
Stable Ct. ME13: Fav 5F **39**
    (off St Mary's Rd.)
Stablegate M. CT2: Cant 5F **39**
    (off St Stephen's Rd.)
Stable M. CT9: Mgte 2H **7**
Staffordshire St. CT11: Ram 3C **6** (2E **37**)
Staines Hill CT2: Sturry 1F 41
Staines Pl. CT10: B'stairs 2H 29
Stancomb Av. CT11: Ram 4C 36
Standard Av. CT6: H Bay 1G 17
Standard Quay ME13: Fav 3F 47
Standard Sq. ME13: Fav 3F 47
Staner Ct. CT12: Ram 1A 36
Stanley Cotts. CT11: Ram 1B **6**
Stanley Gdns. CT6: H Bay 3D 18
Stanley Pl. CT10: B'stairs 3G 29
    CT11: Ram 1B **6** (1E **37**)
    (not continuous)
Stanley Rd. CT5: Whit 6F 15
    CT6: H Bay .3D 18
    CT9: Clift 2A 12
    CT10: B'stairs 1G 29
    CT11: Ram 1A **6** (1D 36)
Stanley Sykes Cl. CT9: Mgte 5B 12
Stanmore Cl. CT1: Cant 3H 43
Staplehurst Av. CT10: B'stairs 5G 29
Staplehurst Gdns. CT9: Clift 2E 13
Star La. CT9: Mgte 2A 28
Starle Cl. CT1: Cant 1H 43
Station App. CT4: Bek 5F 45
    CT5: Whit 4G **15**
    (off Railway Av.)
    CT7: Birch 6D **8**
    CT12: Minst .4G 33
Station App. Rd. CT11: Ram 1A **6** (1C 36)
Station Chine CT6: H Bay 3C 18
Station Pde. CT7: Birch 6D **8**
Station Rd. CT4: Bek, Patr 6F 45
    CT5: Whit 3G 15
    CT6: H Bay .3C 18
    CT7: Birch 6E **9**
    CT8: Wgte S 4A 10
    CT9: Mgte 3F 11
    CT12: Minst .4G 33
    ME13: Fav 5F 47
Station Rd. E. CT1: Cant 6B **4** (3F **43**)
Station Rd. W. CT2: Cant 1E 43
Steam Packet Cotts. CT2: Cant 1F **43**
    (off North La.)
Stephen Cl. CT10: B'stairs 3G 29
Stephens Cl. CT9: Garl 6D 10
    CT11: Ram 1C 36
    ME13: Fav 3D 46
Stephenson Rd. CT10: St Pet 5F 39
Sterling Cl. CT10: St Pet 5E 29
Sterling Ct. CT1: Cant 1C 4
Steven Ct. CT11: Ram 4B 36
Stirling Way CT12: Ram 6H 27
Stockbury Gdns. CT9: Clift 3E 13
Stock Ct. CT2: Cant 4C 38
Stocking Rd. CT10: St Pet 5E 13
Stocks Wlk. CT6: Hern 5F 19
Stockwood Chase CT2: R Comn 6A 38
Stockwood Hill CT2: R Comn 6A 38
Stodmarsh Rd. CT3: Cant, Sturry 2C 44
Stonar Cl. CT11: Ram 6E 29
    CT13: S'wch 4C 48
Stonar Gdns. CT13: S'wch 3C 48
Stone Barn Av. CT7: Birch 1E 25
Stonebridge Rd. CT2: Cant 6G 39
Stonebridge Way ME13: Fav 4D 46
STONE CROSS .6B 48
Stone Cross Lees CT13: S'wch 6B 48
Stonedane Ct. ME13: Fav 3E 47
Stone Gdns. CT10: B'stairs 2H 29
Stone Ho. CT10: B'stairs 6H 13
Stone House Mews CT10: B'stairs 6H 13
Stoneless Golf Course 6D 34
Stone Pier
    Margate 2E **7** (2G 11)
Stone Rd. CT10: B'stairs 2H 29
Stonerock Cl. CT2: Sturry 1F 41

Stone St. ME13: Fav 4E 47
Stour Ct. CT1: Cant 4C 4 (2F 43)
    CT13: S'wch 4B 48
Stour Cres. CT1: Cant 5B 40
Stour M. CT2: Sturry 3D 40
Stour Prom. CT1: Cant 6H 39
Stour Retail Pk. CT1: Cant 5B 40
Stourside Studios CT1: Cant 1F 43
    (off Pound La.)
Stour St. CT1: Cant 5B 4 (2F 43)
Stour Vw. CT2: Cant 6G 39
Stour Vill CT1: Cant 4C 4 (2F 43)
Strand St. CT13: S'wch 3B 48
Strangers Cl. CT1: Cant 4C 42
Strangers La. CT1: Cant 4C 42
Strangford Pl. CT6: Broom 5F 19
Strangford Rd. CT5: Tank 3H 15
Strasbourg St. CT9: Mgte 3F 15
Stream Wlk. CT5: Whit 3F 15
Street, The CT4: Patr 6F 45
    CT7: Acol 4F 25
    CT7: St N 5F 23
    ME13: Oare 1D 46
Streete Ct. CT8: Wgte S 5B 10
Streete Ct. Rd. CT8: Wgte S 5B 10
Streetfield CT6: Hern 6F 19
Stringer Dr. CT7: Birch 1E 25
Strode Pk. Rd. CT6: Hern 5E 19
Stuart Ct. CT1: Cant 4G 43
STUDD HILL 1H 17
Studds Cotts. CT6: H Bay 2G 17
Stuppington Ct. Farm CT4: Cant 6E 43
Stuppington La. CT1: Cant 6E 43
Sturmer Ct. CT1: Cant 2A 44
STURRY 3D 40
Sturry Ct. M. CT2: Sturry 3D 40
Sturry Hill CT2: Sturry 2D 40
Sturry Rd. CT1: Cant 6H 39
    CT2: Cant 6H 39
Sturry Road (Park & Ride) 5B 40
Sturry Station (Rail) 3D 40
Sudbury Pl. CT8: Wgte S 6A 10
Suffolk Av. CT8: Wgte S 6H 9
Suffolk Rd. CT1: Cant 3B 44
Suffolk St. CT5: Whit 5F 15
Sullivan Cl. CT1: Cant 4D 42
Summer Ct. CT2: Harb 1C 42
    CT5: Swale 3C 16
Summerfield Av. CT5: Whit 4H 15
Summerfield Rd. CT9: Clift 3E 13
Summer Hill CT2: Harb 1C 42
Summer La. CT2: T Hill 2E 39
Summer Rd. CT7: St N 6E 23
Sumpter Way ME13: Fav 4B 46
Sunbeam Av. CT6: H Bay 1F 17
Sundew Gro. CT11: Ram 1B 6 (1E 37)
Sundridge Cl. CT2: Cant 4G 39
Sun La. CT7: St N 5F 23
Sunningdale Wlk. CT6: H Bay 6B 18
Sunnyhill Rd. CT6: H Bay 2H 17
Sunnymead CT2: T Hill 1D 38
Sunnyside Cotts. CT2: Sturry 3D 40
Sunnyside Gdns. CT13: S'wch 5A 48
Sunray Av. CT5: Whit 6D 14
Sunset Cl. CT5: Whit 1E 31
Sun St. CT1: Cant 2E 5 (2F 43)
Surrey Cl. CT12: Ram 6B 28
Surrey Gdns. CT7: Birch 6D 8
Surrey Rd. CT1: Cant 3B 44
    CT9: Clift 2B 12
Sussex Av. CT1: Cant 6H 7 (4H 11)
    CT9: Mgte 3A 44
Sussex Cl. CT6: H Bay 1H 17
Sussex Gdns. CT6: H Bay 1H 17
    CT7: Birch 6D 8
    CT8: Wgte S 4B 10
Sussex Mans. CT8: Wgte S 4B 10
    (off Sussex Gdns.)
Sussex St. CT11: Ram 2C 6 (2E 37)
Sussex Wlk. CT1: Cant 3B 44
Sutherland Dr. CT7: Birch 6F 9
Swakeley Wlk. CT5: Swale 2C 16
SWALECLIFFE 3D 16
Swalecliffe Av. CT6: H Bay 1H 17
Swalecliffe Ct. Dr. CT5: Swale 3D 16
Swalecliffe Rd. CT5: Swale, Tank 3A 16
Swale Cl. CT6: Hern 4E 19
Swallow Av. CT5: Whit 1D 30
Swallow Cl. CT9: Mgte 5E 11
Swanfield Rd. CT5: Whit 5F 15
Swanton La. CT3: Sturry 1G 45
Sweechbridge Rd. CT6: H Bay 4B 20
Sweechgate CT2: B Oak 1B 40
Sweyn Rd. CT9: Clift 2A 12
Swinburne Av. CT10: B'stairs 4G 29
Swinford Gdns. CT9: Mgte 5C 12

Sycamore Cl. CT6: Belt 2G 19
    CT9: Mgte 6G 11
    CT10: B'stairs 3C 28
Sycamore Grange CT11: Ram 6F 29
Sydenham St. CT5: Whit 3F 15
Sydney Rd. CT5: Whit 5G 15
    CT11: Ram 1D 6 (1F 37)
Syndale Pl. CT11: Ram 2D 6 (2F 37)

T

Taddy Gdns. CT9: Mgte 5C 12
Talavera Rd. CT1: Cant 2A 44
Talbot Av. CT6: H Bay 2H 17
Talbot Rd. CT9: Mgte 3B 12
Talmead Rd. CT6: H Bay 4E 19
TANKERTON 2A 16
Tankerton Bay Sailing Club 2B 16
Tankerton Cir. CT5: Tank 2H 15
Tankerton Ct. CT5: Tank 2B 16
Tankerton Hgts. CT5: Tank 2G 15
Tankerton M. CT5: Tank 2G 15
    (off Sth. Lodge Cl.)
Tankerton Rd. CT5: Tank 2G 15
Tankerton Slopes 2A 16
Tanners St. ME13: Fav 4E 47
Tanners La. CT13: S'wch 4B 48
Tannery M. CT1: Cant 5B 4 (2F 43)
Tannery Sq. CT1: Cant 4B 4
Tannery Way Nth. CT1: Cant 4B 4 (2E 43)
Tassell's Wlk. CT5: Swale 2D 16
Tavistock Rd. CT11: Ram 6E 29
Taylor Rd. CT12: Minst 3F 33
Teal Dr. CT6: H Bay 5C 18
Teddington Cl. CT1: Cant 6H 39
Telegraph Hill Ind. Est. CT12: Minst 1H 33
Telford Ct. CT6: H Bay 5A 18
Telford M. CT6: H Bay 2C 18
    (off Telford St.)
Telford St. CT6: H Bay 2C 18
Telham Av. CT12: Ram 1B 36
Temeraire Ct. CT9: Mgte 1H 7
Temple Ct. CT2: Cant 1D 42
Temple M. CT1: Cant 4C 4
Temple Rd. CT1: Cant 1D 42
Tennyson Av. CT1: Cant 5B 40
Ten Perch Rd. CT1: Cant 4D 42
Tenterden Dr. CT2: Cant 4F 39
Tenterden Way CT9: Mgte 4C 12
Terminus Dr. CT6: Belt 2H 19
Terrace, The CT2: Cant 5F 39
    ME13: Fav 4C 46
Terry's La. CT5: Whit 3F 15
Teynham Cl. CT9: Clift 3F 13
Teynham Dr. CT5: Whit 3H 15
Teynham Rd. CT5: Whit 3H 15
Thanet Cl. CT10: B'stairs 2H 29
Thanet Crematorium CT9: Mgte 6G 11
Thanet Ent. Cen. CT10: St Pet 6D 12
Thanet Indoor Bowls Cen. 2B 12
Thanet Pl. CT10: B'stairs 1H 29
Thanet Pl. Gdns. CT10: B'stairs 1H 29
Thanet Reach Bus. Pk.
    CT10: B'stairs 3C 28
Thanet Rd. CT8: Wgte S 4H 9
    CT9: Mgte 4H 7 (3H 11)
    CT10: B'stairs 3H 29
    CT11: Ram 1D 6 (2F 37)
Thanet Way CT5: Ches, Whit 2D 30
    CT6: H Bay, M'side 5E 19
    CT7: St N 4A 22
    ME13: Hernh 5A 30
Thanet Way Retail Pk.
    CT5: Ches 4C 16
Thanington Ct. CT1: Cant 4C 42
Thanington Rd. CT1: Cant 4C 42
THANINGTON WITHOUT 4C 42
The . . . .
    Names prefixed with 'The' for example
    'The Arcadian' are indexed under the
    main name such as 'Arcadian, The'
Theatre Royal
    Margate 3G 7
Third Av. CT9: Clift 2B 12
Thirlmere Av. CT11: Ram 2A 36
Thistle Dr. CT5: Whit 2D 30
Thomas Neame Av. ME13: Fav 4G 47
Thomas Rd. ME13: Fav 4E 47
Thornden Cl. CT6: H Bay 3G 17
Thornden Ct. CT2: Cant 4C 38
Thornden Wood Rd. CT6: H Bay 6D 18
THORNE .3B 34
Thorne Hill CT12: Ram 2B 34
Thorne Rd. CT12: Minst 3F 33
Thorn Gdns. CT11: Ram 6E 29

Thornhurst CT6: Belt 3H 19
Three Kings Yd. CT13: S'wch 4C 48
Throwley Cotts. CT9: Garl 6D 10
Throwley Dr. CT6: H Bay 3A 18
Thrupp Paddock CT10: B'stairs 4G 13
Thundersland Rd. CT6: H Bay 3F 19
    (not continuous)
Thurlow Av. CT6: Belt 2G 19
THURSTON PARK 4G 15
Thurston Pk. CT5: Whit 4G 15
Thwaytes Ct. CT6: H Bay 3B 18
Tidewell M. CT8: Wgte S 5A 10
Tile Kiln Hill CT7: Blean 3B 38
Tina Gdns. CT10: B'stairs 1G 29
Tinbridge Oast ME13: Fav 6H 47
Tin Shop Hill ME13: Fav 2B 46
Tippledore La. CT10: St Pet 2E 29
Tivoli Brooks CT9: Mgte 6F 7 (4G 11)
Tivoli Pk. Av. CT9: Mgte 6E 7 (4F 11)
Tivoli Rd. CT9: Mgte 6F 7 (5G 11)
Tollemache Ct. CT12: Mans 5B 26
Tollgate Cl. CT5: Whit 5E 15
Tomlin Dr. CT9: Mgte 5C 12
Tomson's Pas. CT11: Ram 3A 6 (2D 36)
Tom Thumb Theatre
    Margate 2B 12
Tonford La. CT1: Cant 4B 42
    CT2: Harb 2A 42
Tothill St. CT12: Minst 3F 33
Tourist Info. Cen.
    Canterbury 2D 4 (2F 43)
    Faversham 4F 47
    Herne Bay 2D 17
    Margate 2F 7 (2G 11)
    Ramsgate 4D 6 (3F 37)
    Sandwich 4B 48
Tourtel Rd. CT1: Cant 1G 43
Tower Bungs. CT7: Birch 5E 9
Tower Hill CT5: Tank 2G 15
Tower House
    Canterbury 1B 4
Tower Pde. CT5: Whit 2G 15
Tower Rd. CT5: Whit 3G 15
Tower Way CT1: Cant 2B 4 (2F 43)
Town Ct. CT6: H Bay 2D 17
    (off High St.)
Townley St. CT11: Ram 5A 6 (3D 36)
Tradewinds CT5: Whit 1D 30
Trafalgar M. CT11: Ram 5A
    (off Royal Rd.)
Trafalgar Rd. CT7: Wdchu 4B 2
Trenley Dr. CT3: Cant 1D 4
Trilby Way CT5: Whit 1D 3
Trinity Ct. CT9: Mgte 2G 7 (2H 11)
    CT11: Ram 3D
Trinity Hill CT9: Mgte 2H 1
    (off Trinity Sq.)
Trinity Pl. CT11: Ram 2D 6 (2F 37)
Trinity Sq. CT9: Mgte 2G 7 (2H 11)
    CT10: B'stairs 6F 1
Trinity Wlk. CT9: Mgte 2G
Trotwood Pl. CT10: B'stairs 3H 2
    (off Sea App)
Troughton M. CT9: Mgte 4F 1
Trove Ct. CT11: Ram 3D
Trueman Ct. CT2: Blean 2H
Truro Rd. CT11: Ram 3D 6 (2F 37)
Tudor Cl. CT7: Birch 5F
Tudor Ct. CT2: Cant 4C 3
    CT5: Tank 2A 1
Tudor House
    Margate 2G 7 (2H 11)
Tudor Rd. CT1: Cant 3E 4
Tunhouse, The ME13: Fav 3F 4
    (off Court St
Tunis Ct. CT1: Cant 1B 4
Tunis Row CT10: B'stairs 2H 2
Tunstall Rd. CT2: Cant 4G 3
Turnagain La. CT1: Cant 2E 5 (2F 43)
Turnden Gdns. CT9: Clift 3E 1
Turner Contemporary 2F 7 (2G 11
Turner Ct. CT9: Mgte 3A 1
Turner Hgts. CT9: Mgte 5C
Turner St. CT11: Ram 4C 6 (2E 37)
Turnstones Ct. CT8: Wgte S 4A 1
    (off Westgate Bay Av
Two Chimneys Holiday Pk.
    CT7: Birch 2H 2
Twyne Ct. CT2: Sturry 3D 4
Tydemans Av. CT5: Ches 4C 1
Tyler Cl. CT2: Cant 4E 3
Tyler Ct. CT2: Cant 4E 3
TYLER HILL 2E 3
Tyler Hill Rd. CT2: Blean, T Hill 2E 3
Tyler Way CT5: Swale 2E 1
Tyler Way Ind. Est. CT5: Swale 2E 1

Tyndale Pk. CT6: H Bay 3F 19
Tyson Av. CT9: Mgte 4C 10

U

UCA Canterbury 3H 43
Ulcombe Gdns. CT2: Cant 5G 39
Ulster Rd. CT9: Mgte 6G 7 (5H 11)
Underdown La. CT6: H Bay 4D 18
Underdown Pas. CT2: Cant 3E 43
Underdown Rd. CT6: H Bay 2D 18
UNDER THE WOOD 5D 20
Underwood Cl. CT4: Cant 5G 43
Union Cres.
  CT9: Mgte 3F 7 (3G 11)
Union Pl. CT1: Cant 1G 43
Union Rd. CT11: Ram 1D 6 (1F 37)
Union Row CT9: Mgte 3F 7 (3H 11)
Union Sq. CT10: B'stairs 3H 29
Union St. CT1: Cant 1G 43
  CT11: Ram 3C 6 (2E 37)
  ME13: Fav 4E 47
Unity Pl. CT11: Ram 2D 6 (2F 37)
University of Kent
  Canterbury Campus 4E 39
University Rd. CT2: Cant 5D 38
Upchurch Wlk. CT9: Clift 4E 13
Uplands CT2: Cant 4F 39
Uplees Rd. ME13: Oare 1C 46
Up. Approach Rd. CT10: B'stairs 4G 29
Up. Balcomb M. CT9: Mgte 5C 12
                      (off Balcomb Cres.)
Up. Brents ME13: Fav 3F 47
Up. Bridge St. CT1: Cant 6F 5 (3G 43)
Up. Chantry La. CT1: Cant 6H 5 (3G 43)
Up. Dane Rd. CT9: Mgte 4A 12
Up. Dumpton Pk. Rd. CT11: Ram ..2B 6 (1E 37)
Up. Free Down CT6: Hern 5F 19
Upper Grounds CT3: H Bay, Hoath ...5C 20
Up. Gro. CT9: Mgte 3G 7 (3H 11)
Upper Hale CT7: St N 3A 24
UPPER HARBLEDOWN 1A 42
Up. Maltings Pl. CT7: Birch 6D 8
Up. St Ann's Rd. ME13: Fav 5D 46
Up. Strand St. CT13: S'wch 4C 48
UPTON 3E 29
Upton Grange CT10: B'stairs 3F 29
Upton Rd. CT10: St Pet 2F 29
Ursuline Dr. CT8: Wgte S 6H 9

V

Vale, The CT10: B'stairs 3F 29
Vale Ct. CT11: Ram 5A 6
Vale Pl. CT11: Ram 3D 36
Vale Rd. CT5: Whit 5F 15
  CT10: B'stairs 3F 29
  CT11: Ram 4A 6 (3C 36)
Vale Sq. CT11: Ram 5A 6 (3D 36)
Valkyrie Av. CT5: Whit 6D 14
Valley Rd. CT1: Cant 4E 43
  CT9: Mgte 3G 27
Vauxhall Av. CT1: Cant 5A 40
  CT6: H Bay 2G 17
Vauxhall Cres. CT1: Cant 5A 40
Vauxhall Ind. Est. CT1: Cant 4A 40
Vauxhall Ind. Rd. CT1: Cant 4B 40
Vauxhall Lakes Nature Reserve 5H 39
Vauxhall Rd. CT1: Cant 4A 40
Ventnor La. CT9: Mgte 4G 7 (3H 11)
Vere Rd. CT10: B'stairs 3G 29
Vereth Rd. CT11: Ram 3D 36
Vernon Pl. CT1: Cant 6G 5 (3G 43)
Verwood Cl. CT2: Cant 6E 39
Vestey Ct. CT8: Wgte S 4A 10
Viaduct Cl. CT12: Ram 1C 36
Vicarage Cres. CT9: Mgte 6G 7 (4H 11)
Vicarage Gdn. CT12: Monk'n 2A 32
Vicarage Gdns. CT5: Whit 5F 15
Vicarage La. CT2: Blean 2A 38
  CT13: S'wch 4B 48
  ME13: Osp 6C 46
Vicarage Pl. CT9: Mgte 5F 7 (4H 11)
Vicarage St. CT10: St Pet 2D 28
  ME13: Fav 3F 47
Victor Av. CT9: Clift 3D 12
Victoria Av. CT2: Cant 2E 43
  CT8: Wgte S 6B 10
  CT9: Mgte 4B 12
  CT10: St Pet 5E 13
Victoria Ct. CT9: Mgte 4E 11
  CT11: Ram 2D 6
Victoria Dr. CT6: H Bay 2A 18
Victoria Ho. CT11: Ram 4D 6

Victoria M. CT5: Whit 3F 15
                         (off Bexley St.)
  CT11: Ram 2D 6
Victoria Pde. CT10: B'stairs 4H 29
  CT11: Ram 2F 37
Victoria Pk. CT6: H Bay 2D 18
Victoria Pl. ME13: Fav 4E 47
Victoria Rd. CT1: Cant 3E 43
  CT9: Mgte 5G 7 (4H 11)
                         (Portland Rd.)
  CT9: Mgte 5G 7 (4H 11)
                         (St Peter's Rd.)
  CT10: St Pet 1E 29
  CT11: Ram 2D 6 (2F 37)
Victoria Row CT1: Cant 1G 43
  CT11: Ram 4C 36
Victoria St. CT5: Whit 3F 15
Victoria Walk, The CT1: Cant 1D 4
Victoria Yd. CT1: Cant 1G 43
                         (off Victoria Row)
Viking Cl. CT7: Birch 5B 8
Viking Ct. CT2: Cant 6F 39
                         (off St Stephen's Cl.)
  CT9: Mgte 3A 12
  CT10: B'stairs 4H 29
Viking Ship (Hugin) 4G 35
Villiers Ho. CT10: B'stairs 6H 13
Villiers Rd. CT1: Cant 1B 44
Vincent Cl. CT10: B'stairs 4C 28
Vincent Farm M. CT9: Mgte 5E 27
Vincent Rd. CT9: Mgte 3E 27
Vine Cl. CT11: Ram 5E 29
Vine End CT11: Ram 5E 29
Violet Av. CT12: Ram 5C 28
Virginia Rd. CT5: Whit 5A 16
Viscount Sq. CT6: H Bay 4E 19
Vue Cinema
  Ramsgate 3A 28
Vulcan Cl. CT5: Whit 6E 15
Vyeson Ct. CT11: Ram 4B 6

W

Wacher Cl. CT2: Cant 6F 39
Wacher Ct. CT6: H Bay 2D 18
Walcot Pl. CT6: Hern 4F 19
Walden Ct. CT2: Cant 5G 39
Waldron Rd. CT10: B'stairs 5H 29
Walker La. CT7: Birch 5B 8
Wallace Way CT10: B'stairs 3E 29
Wallers Rd. ME13: Fav 4C 46
Walley World
  Margate 4E 7 (3G 11)
Wallis Ct. CT6: Belt 2B 20
Wallwood Rd. CT11: Ram 1F 37
Walmer Gdns. CT12: C'snd 4E 35
Walmer Rd. CT5: Whit 5G 15
Walmsley Rd. CT10: St Pet 2F 29
Walnut Cl. CT10: B'stairs 5F 29
Walnut M. CT7: Birch 6D 8
Walnut Tree Cl. CT7: Birch 6E 9
Walnut Tree La. CT2: West 1H 41
Walpole Bay Hotel Mus. 2B 12
Walpole Rd. CT9: Mgte 3G 7 (2H 11)
Waltham Cl. CT9: Clift 3E 13
Wansum Ct. CT7: St N 5F 23
Wantsum Cl. CT6: Belt 2B 20
Wantsume Lees CT13: S'wch 3A 48
Wantsum M. CT13: S'wch 4B 48
Wantsum Way CT7: St N 5E 23
Warden Point Way CT5: Whit 1E 31
Wardour Cl. CT10: B'stairs 3H 29
Warre Av. CT11: Ram 4C 36
Warren, The CT5: Whit 1E 31
Warren Dr. CT10: St Pet 2E 29
Warren Drive, The CT8: Wgte S 6H 9
Warten Rd. CT11: Ram 6F 29
Warwick Dr. CT11: Ram 4B 36
Warwick M. CT11: Ram 5A 6
Warwick Rd. CT1: Cant 2A 44
  CT5: Whit 3F 15
  CT9: Clift 3B 12
Watchester Av. CT11: Ram 4C 36
Watchester La. CT12: Minst 4F 33
Water La. CT1: Cant 3C 4 (2F 43)
  CT2: Sturry 3D 40
  ME13: Fav 4E 47
                         (off Partridge La.)
  ME13: Osp 6C 46
Waterloo Pl. CT11: Ram 3D 6 (2F 37)
Waterloo Rd. CT5: Whit 3F 15
Water Mdws. CT2: Ford 4D 40
Waters Edge CT1: Cant 6H 39
Waterside Cl. ME13: Fav 2F 47
Waterside Dr. CT8: Wgte S 4B 10

Waterstone Pl. ME13: Fav 5C 46
                         (off Grove Cl.)
Waterways Caravan Pk. CT6: Rec ...1E 21
Watling St. CT1: Cant 4D 4 (2F 43)
Watts Yd. CT13: S'wch 4B 48
                         (off Cattle Mkt.)
Wauchope Rd. CT5: Seas 1B 30
Wave Crest CT5: Whit 4E 15
Waverley Rd. CT9: Mgte 4D 10
WAY 2A 34
Wayborough Hill CT12: Minst 2H 33
Wayfares CT13: S'wch 6B 48
Way Hill CT12: Minst 3H 33
Wayne Cl. CT10: St Pet 2E 29
Wayside Caravan Pk. CT12: Minst ..3A 34
Wealdhurst Pk. CT10: St Pet 2D 28
Weatherly Dr. CT10: B'stairs 5F 29
Weigall Pl. CT11: Ram 2C 36
Weighbridge Cotts. CT2: Cant 1F 43
Weir Ct. CT1: Cant 6H 39
Well Cl. CT2: Sturry 2E 41
Wellesley Cl. CT8: Wgte S 6A 10
  CT10: B'stairs 4F 29
Wellesley Ct. CT11: Ram 3C 6
Wellesley Rd. CT8: Wgte S 6B 10
  CT9: Mgte 4B 12
Wellesley Ter. CT13: S'wch 5C 48
Wellington Cl. CT8: Wgte S 4A 10
Wellington Cres. CT11: Ram ...4D 6 (3F 37)
Wellington Gdns. CT9: Mgte ..2H 7 (2H 11)
Wellington Rd. CT8: Wgte S 2A 10
Wellington St. CT5: Whit 2F 31
Wellis Gdns. CT9: Mgte 4E 11
Well La. CT2: Ford 5E 41
Wells Av. CT1: Cant 3H 43
Wells Way ME13: Fav 2D 46
Welsdene Rd. CT9: Garl 5C 10
Wemyss Way CT1: Cant 1A 44
Wentworth Av. CT9: Mgte 4C 10
Wentworth Dr. CT12: Ram 6A 28
Wentworth Gdns. CT6: H Bay 5B 18
West Beach CT5: Whit 4E 15
West Beach Caravan Pk. CT5: Whit ..5D 14
WESTBERE 1G 41
Westbere Frostbite Sailing Club ...2G 41
Westbere La. CT2: West 2F 41
Westbere Sailing Opportunities ...3E 41
WESTBROOK 4E 11
Westbrook Av. CT9: Mgte 4B 10
Westbrook Cotts. CT9: Mgte 4E 11
Westbrook Gdns. CT9: Mgte 4E 11
Westbrook Ind. Est. CT6: H Bay 2H 17
Westbrook La. CT6: H Bay 2H 17
Westbrook Prom. CT9: Mgte 3C 10
Westbrook Rd. CT9: Mgte 3E 11
Westbury Rd. CT8: Wgte S 5A 10
West Cliff CT5: Whit 5E 15
Westcliff Arc. CT11: Ram 5B 6 (3E 37)
West Cliff Av. CT10: B'stairs 4H 29
West Cliff Ct. CT10: B'stairs 4H 29
                         (off West Cliff Rd.)
West Cliff Dr. CT6: H Bay 1H 17
West Cliff Gdns. CT6: H Bay 1H 17
Westcliff Gdns. CT9: Mgte 4D 10
West Cliff Mans. CT11: Ram 4B 6
                         (off West Cliff St.)
West Cliff M. CT10: B'stairs 4H 29
                         (off West Cliff Rd.)
West Cliff Prom. CT10: B'stairs 5H 29
  CT11: Ram 6A 6 (4D 36)
West Cliff Rd. CT10: B'stairs 4G 29
  CT11: Ram 5A 6 (3D 36)
Westcliff Rd. CT9: Mgte 4E 11
West Cliff Ter. CT11: Ram 4B 36
Westcliff Ter. Mans. CT11: Ram 4B 36
WEST DUMPTON 6E 29
W. Dumpton La. CT11: Ram 5E 29
WEST END 5G 17
Westerham Cl. CT2: Cant 4G 39
  CT9: Clift 4F 13
Westerly M. CT2: Cant 1E 43
Western Av. CT6: H Bay 3B 18
Western Esplanade CT6: H Bay 2A 18
  CT10: B'stairs 5H 29
Western Link ME13: Fav 4B 46
Western Rd. CT9: Mgte 5C 12
Western Undercliff CT11: Ram 4D 36
                         (off Royal Harbour App.)
Westfield CT2: Blean 2A 38
Westfield Cotts. CT2: Ford 4D 40
Westfield Rd. CT7: Birch 6D 8
  CT9: Garl, Mgte 5D 10
Westgate & Birchington Golf Course ..5H 9
Westgate Av. CT7: Wdchu 3C 26
Westgate Bay Av. CT8: Wgte S 4H 9
Westgate Cl. CT2: Cant 1C 42

Westgate Ct. Av. CT2: Cant 1C 42
Westgate Gdn. Flats CT1: Cant 2A 4 (2E 43)
Westgate Gro. CT2: Cant 1A 4 (1F 43)
Westgate Hall Rd. CT1: Cant 1C 4 (1F 43)
WESTGATE ON SEA 4A 10
Westgate-on-Sea Station (Rail) 4A 10
Westgate Pavilion & Theatre 3A 10
Westgate Pl. ME13: Fav 4G 47
Westgate Ter. CT5: Whit 3G 15
Westgate Towers
   Canterbury 1B 4 (1F 43)
West Hill Rd. CT6: H Bay 2A 18
Westlands Rd. CT6: H Bay 4A 18
Westleigh Rd. CT8: Wgte S 5H 9
Westmarsh Dr. CT9: Clift 3E 13
Westmeads Rd. CT5: Whit 3G 15
Westminster Rd. CT1: Cant 4A 40
Westminster Wlk. CT12: Ram 6C 28
Westonville Av. CT9: Mgte 4D 10
Westover Gdns. CT10: St Pet 6E 13
Westover Rd. CT10: St Pet 6E 13
West Pk. Av. CT9: Mgte 4D 12
West Pl. CT2: Cant 1E 43
West Ri. CT12: Ram 6B 28
West St. ME13: Fav 4E 47
West Vw. Cl. CT6: H Bay 5A 18
WESTWOOD 2A 28
Westwood Cross CT10: B'stairs 3A 28
Westwood Dr. CT2: Cant 6G 39
Westwood Gateway Retail Pk.
   CT10: B'stairs .2A 28
Westwood Ind. Est. CT9: Mgte 1A 28
Westwood Pl. ME13: Fav 6F 47
Westwood Retail Pk. CT10: B'stairs 2B 28
Westwood Rd. CT10: B'stairs 3B 28
Weyburn Dr. CT12: Ram 6A 28
Weyman Ter. CT6: H Bay 4E 19
Wharfedale Rd. CT9: Mgte 5H 7 (4A 12)
Whatmer Cl. CT2: Sturry 2E 41
Wheatley Pl. CT9: Mgte 5G 7
Wheatley Rd. CT5: Whit 3G 15
   CT12: Ram 6C 28
Wheler Ct. ME13: Fav 4C 46
Wherry Cl. CT9: Mgte 2A 28
Whinfell Av. CT11: Ram 2H 35
Whitbourne Ct. CT5: Whit 5F 15
Whitefriars Mdw. CT13: S'wch 5B 48
Whitefriars Pas. CT1: Cant 5F 5
Whitefriars Shop. Cen. CT1: Cant . . .4E 5 (2F 43)
Whitefriars Sq. CT1: Cant 5E 5
Whitefriars St. CT1: Cant 5F 5 (2G 43)
Whitefriars Way CT13: S'wch 4B 48
WHITEHALL 6B 28
Whitehall Bri. Rd. CT2: Cant 2A 4 (1E 43)
Whitehall Cl. CT2: Cant 2A 4 (2E 43)
Whitehall Gdns. CT2: Cant 1A 4 (1E 43)
Whitehall Rd. CT2: Cant 2A 4 (3C 42)
   CT12: Ram 1B 36
White Hart Mans. CT9: Mgte 2F 7
White Horse La. CT1: Cant 3D 4 (2F 43)
White Marsh Rd. CT5: Whit 3G 15
White Mill Rural Heritage Cen. 3A 48
Whiteness Grn. CT10: B'stairs 4F 13
Whiteness Rd. CT10: B'stairs 4G 13
Whitepost CT5: Whit 3F 15
   (off Horsebridge Rd.)
Whitfield Av. CT10: St Pet 6E 13
Whitgift Ct. CT2: Cant 1D 42
Whiting Cres. ME13: Fav 3C 46
WHITSTABLE 3F 15
Whitstable & Seasalter Golf Course 4E 15
WHITSTABLE & TANKERTON HOSPITAL 3A 16
Whitstable Castle .2G 15
Whitstable Harbour 2F 15
Whitstable Mus. & Gallery 4F 15
Whitstable Oyster Yawl 'Favourite' 3E 15
Whitstable Rd. CT2: Blean, Cant 4B 38
   (not continuous)
   CT6: H Bay 2F 17
   ME13: Fav 4G 47
Whitstable Sports Cen. 5H 15
Whitstable Station (Rail) 4G 15

Whitstable Swimming Pool 2F 15
Whitstable Yacht Club 3F 15
Whytecliffs CT10: B'stairs 5G 29
Wichling Cl. CT2: Cant 5G 39
Wicketts End CT5: Whit 5F 15
Wickham Av. CT11: Ram 1G 37
Wife of Bath Hill CT2: Cant 2C 42
Wigwam Paddocks CT7: Birch 5E 9
Wilbrough Rd. CT7: Birch 6E 9
Wilderness Hill CT9: Mgte 3H 7 (3A 12)
Wildish Rd. ME13: Fav 3C 46
Wildwood Rd. CT2: Sturry 2D 40
Wilfred Rd. CT11: Ram 2C 36
Wilkes Rd. CT10: B'stairs 4E 29
Wilkie Rd. CT7: Birch 5E 9
Willement Rd. ME13: Fav 4D 46
Willetts Hill CT12: Monk'n 2B 32
William Av. CT9: Mgte 5C 12
William Gibbs Ct. ME13: Fav 4F 47
William Ho. CT9: Mgte 4G 7
   (off Princes Cres.)
William St. CT5: Whit 3F 15
   CT6: H Bay 3D 18
   ME13: Fav 4F 47
Willoughby Ct. CT1: Cant 5D 4 (2F 43)
Willow Av. CT10: B'stairs 3D 28
   ME13: Fav 4C 46
Willowbank CT13: S'wch 4C 48
Willowbrook Cl. CT6: H Bay 4E 19
Willow Cl. CT2: Cant 6G 39
   CT9: Mgte 3C 12
   CT5: Whit 5G 15
   CT10: St Pet 2F 29
Willow Farm Way CT6: Broom 5G 19
Willow M. CT6: Hern 6E 19
Willow Rd. CT5: Whit 2E 31
Willows, The CT6: H Bay 3B 18
Willows Ct. CT2: Cant 4C 38
Willow Tree Cl. CT6: Belt 2H 19
Willow Way CT5: Ches 5C 16
   CT9: Mgte 5E 11
Willson's Rd. CT11: Ram 3C 36
Wilson's M. CT11: Ram 3D 36
   (off Wilson's Rd.)
Wilton Rd. CT12: Ram 6H 27
Wimborne Pl. CT12: Ram 1B 36
Wincheap CT1: Cant 4D 42
Wincheap (Park & Ride) 4D 42
Wincheap Green 6B 4 (3E 43)
Wincheap Ind. Est. CT1: Cant 3D 42
Wincheap Retail Pk. CT1: Cant 3E 43
Winchester Gdns. CT1: Cant 4G 43
Windermere ME13: Fav 5G 47
Windermere Av. CT11: Ram 2H 35
Windmill Av. CT12: Ram 4B 28
Windmill Cl. CT1: Cant 2A 44
   CT6: Hern 5E 19
Windmill Ct. CT5: Whit 6E 15
Windmill La. ME13: Fav 2D 46
Windmill Pl. CT11: Ram 3C 36
   (off Cannonbury Rd.)
Windmill Rd. CT1: Cant 2A 44
   CT5: Whit 6F 15
   CT6: Hern 5E 19
Windmill Vw. CT9: Mgte 5A 12
Windmill Wlk. CT12: Ram 6B 28
Windsor Av. CT9: Mgte 4B 12
Windsor Cl. CT10: St Pet 2E 29
Windsor Ct. CT9: Mgte 4B 12
Windsor Gdns. CT6: H Bay 2F 17
Windsor Ho. CT5: Whit 4F 15
Windsor M. CT9: Mgte 4G 7
   (off St John's St.)
Windsor Rd. CT1: Cant 4C 42
   CT12: C'snd 2F 35
Wingate Hill CT2: Harb 1A 42
Wings Cl. CT10: B'stairs 2H 29
Wings Ct. CT10: B'stairs 2H 29
Winifred Av. CT12: Ram 5C 28
Winkle Cl. CT6: H Bay 2H 17
Winstanley Cres. CT11: Ram 1A 6 (1D 36)
Winston Cl. CT1: Cant 3A 44
Winston Ct. CT7: Birch 5E 9

Winston Gdns. CT6: Belt 3H 19
Winter Gardens
   Margate 1G 7 (2H 11)
Winterstoke Cres. CT11: Ram 1G 37
Winterstoke Undercliff CT11: Ram 2G 37
Winterstoke Way CT11: Ram 1F 37
Wolseley Av. CT6: H Bay 1G 17
WOODCHURCH 2B 26
Woodchurch Rd. CT7: Wdchu 4B 26
   CT9: Wdchu 2B 26
Woodcote CT5: Ches 4D 16
Woodford Av. CT12: Ram 6D 28
Woodford Ct. CT7: Birch 6E 9
Woodgate Cl. ME13: Fav 3E 47
Wood Hill CT2: T Hill 2E 39
Woodland Av. CT7: Birch 1F 25
Woodland Rd. CT6: H Bay 3H 17
Woodland Way CT2: Cant 4D 38
   CT10: B'stairs .4G 13
Woodlawn St. CT5: Whit 3F 15
Woodman Av. CT5: Swale 2D 16
Woodnesborough Rd.
   CT13: S'wch 6A 48
Woodrow Chase CT6: Hern 6E 19
Woodside Rd. CT2: Sturry 1D 40
Woodvale Av. CT5: Ches 5C 16
Woodville Cl. CT1: Cant 4D 42
Woodville Rd. CT12: Ram 6C 28
Woolf College CT2: Cant 3E 39
Woollets Cl. CT6: H Bay 4A 18
Woolmer Cl. CT1: Cant 4H 43
Worcester Cl. ME13: Fav 5G 47
Worcester Gro. CT10: St Pet 1F 29
Worcester La. CT3: Cant 3C 44
Worthgate Pl. CT1: Cant 6C 4 (3F 43)
Wotton Ct. CT7: St N 5F 23
Wraik Hill CT5: Whit 3D 30
   (not continuous)
Wraik Hill & Foxes Cross Local Nature Reserve
   . . . . .3D 30
Wreight Ct. ME13: Fav 2D 46
Wrentham Av. CT6: H Bay 3H 17
Wrotham Av. CT10: B'stairs 3H 29
Wrotham Cres. CT10: B'stairs 4G 29
Wrotham Rd. CT10: B'stairs 3H 29
Wyards Print and Artworks Ltd. 5D 46
   (off Ospringe Rd.)
Wye Gdns. CT9: Clift 3F 13
Wye Grn. CT6: H Bay 4D 18
Wyndham Av. CT9: Mgte 3B 12
Wynn Ellis Ho. CT5: Whit 2G 15
   (off Tower Pde.)
Wynn Rd. CT5: Tank 2A 16

Y

Yardhurst Gdns. CT9: Clift 2F 13
Yardley Ho. CT10: B'stairs 6H 13
Yarrow Cl. CT10: B'stairs 4G 29
Yeomans Dr. CT2: Cant 2C 42
Yew Tree Cl. CT10: B'stairs 3D 28
Yew Tree Gdns. CT2: Ford 4E 41
   CT7: Birch 6E 9
Yoakley Sq. CT9: Mgte 5H 11
York Av. CT10: B'stairs 3H 29
York Cl. CT6: H Bay 3B 18
YORKLETTS 4C 30
York Rd. CT1: Cant 3E 43
   CT6: H Bay 2B 18
York St. CT10: B'stairs 3H 29
   CT11: Ram 4C 6 (3E 37)
York Street Gallery 4C 6
York Ter. CT7: Birch 6F 9
   CT11: Ram 4B 6
   (off Westcliff Arc.)
Ypres Ct. CT1: Cant 1B 43

Z

Zealand Rd. CT1: Cant 4F 43
Zion Pl. CT9: Mgte 2H 7 (2H 11)

GUIDE TO SELECTED PLACES OF INTEREST

HOW TO USE THE GUIDE

Opening times for places of interest vary considerably depending on the season, day of the week or the ownership of the property. Please check opening times before starting your journey.

The index reference is to the square in which the place of interest appears. e.g. **Canterbury Cathedral** 2F **5**, is to be found in square 2F on page 5.

EH, English Heritage

CANTERBURY

Canterbury has emerged from its early beginnings as a Roman settlement to become a popular tourist destination and place of Christian pilgrimage for people all over the world.

Undoubtably Canterbury's most commanding and significant feature is the Cathedral with its magnificent tower and history dating back to Anglo-Saxon times. Named as one of Britain's Heritage cities, it is also notable for historical architecture such as the Roman Quenin Gate, the Norman Castle, Westgate Towers and the fragmented remains of the city walls. In addition to the Cathedral, Canterbury also boasts a further two UNESCO World Heritage sites, St. Augustine's Abbey and St. Martin's Church.

Associations with noted figures such as the first Archbishop, St. Augustine, the martyred Thomas Becket and 'father of English literature', Geoffrey Chaucer have only added to Canterbury's rich historical and literary heritage.

Present day visitors will find much to enjoy and explore with a wide range of tourist attractions, fine restaurants, unique shops and welcoming pubs.

Canterbury Cathedral

ℹ️ Tourist and Visitor Information Centres

Canterbury, The Beaney, 18 High Street, CT1 2RA. Tel: 01227 378100. 2D **4**

Faversham, Fleur de Lis Heritage Centre, 13 Preston Street, ME13 8NS. Tel: 01795 534542. 4F **47**

Herne Bay, Herne Bay Office, William Street, CT6 5NX. Tel: 01227 378100. 2D **18**

Sandwich, (Summer only), Guildhall, Cattle Market, CT13 9AH. Tel: 01304 613565. 4B **48**

Thanet, The Droit House, Stone Pier, Margate, CT9 1JD. Tel: 01843 577577. Providing visitor information for Margate, Broadstairs and Ramsgate. 2F **7**

scan these QR codes for :

www.canterbury.co.uk

www.visitthanet.co.uk

Beaney, The 2D 4

(Also known as Canterbury Royal Museum)
18 High Street. Tel: 01227 378100.
The Beaney House of Art and Knowledge displays a wide range of artifacts from ancient cultures together with natural history, paintings and drawings.

Blean Woods National Nature Reserve 4A 38

Rough Common Road, Rough Common, Canterbury. Tel: 01227 455972.
This is the largest area of ancient broadleaved woodland in southern Britain and contains a wide selection of tree species including oak, beech, hazel and hornbeam. The woodland floor is littered with bluebells in the spring, with bracken predominating otherwise. This abundance of different vegetation provides habitats for birds such as woodpecker, nightingale, nuthatch and nightjar among others, whilst within the wide rides glimpses of the rare heath fritillary butterfly and seven-spot ladybird may be obtained along with sightings of rare orchid and St John's wort. The flora and fauna may also be enjoyed by using the five woodland trails, some of which are wheelchair and pushchair friendly.

Canterbury Cathedral 2F 5

Burgate. Tel: 01227 762862.
The centre of the Anglican church and seat of the Archbishop of Canterbury, the origins of the cathedral date back to 597 AD when St Augustine arrived in Britain to convert the resident Angles to Christianity. Over the centuries the building increased in size and stature, formally becoming a Benedictine monastery in the late 10th century and being completely rebuilt by the Normans following the conquest of 1066. After the murder of Archbishop Thomas Becket in 1170, his shrine became a place of international pilgrimage, the income from this subsidising further building. It ceased to be a monastery in 1540 during the Dissolution by Henry VIII. The last major work occurred during the 1830s when the North West tower was rebuilt as a copy of that of the South West and the cathedral became effectively as it is seen today. Famous also for its stained glass, Canterbury Cathedral has many surviving examples from the 12th and 13th centuries as well as important 19th and 20th century pieces. The Cathedral is a living, working church with a full-time staff of 250 and conducting over 100 services a year.

Canterbury Environment Centre 1E 5

St. Alphege Lane.
Tel: 01227 457009.
Located in a former church dating from the 1070s, the centre is dedicated to the study of the history and culture of Canterbury and plays host to events and exhibitions detailing the past, present and future of this historic city.

Canterbury Environmental Education Centre 5H 39

Broad Oak Road. Tel: 01227 452 447.
Located in the city of Canterbury, these 30 acres of woodland, lakes and grassland are an urban oasis for wildlife and home to dormice, bats, kingfishers and heron as well as being a haven for rare orchids and other flora. Trails, bird hides and a sensory garden allow the visitor to come close to nature. Educational and fun, the centre caters for school and university groups throughout the year and for the general public during the summer term holidays.

Canterbury Heritage Museum 3C 4

Stour Street. Tel: 01227 475202.
A fine medieval timbered building dated 1373. Originally a hospital for poor priests, now housing displays showing the history of the city from pre-Roman times to the present. There are hands-on activities for children, a Bagpuss and Clangers display and the story of Rupert Bear.

Canterbury Norman Castle 6B 4

Castle Street.
The castles of Dover, Rochester and Canterbury were built as a direct result of the Norman invasions of 1066 as the need for impenetrable fortresses became critical. The imposing keep of Canterbury Castle replaced the motte & bailey structure at nearby Dane John and acted out its purpose until the 13th century, when it became a jail. In Victorian times it was a storage centre for gas, losing its roof in the process. In 1928 the council rescued the site from centuries of neglect and demolition by restoring the remaining shell of the keep.

Canterbury Roman Museum 3F 5

Butchery Lane. Tel: 01227 785575.
Situated underground at the level of the old Roman Town, Durovernum Cantiacorum, the museum houses a fine collection of excavated Roman artefacts and contains the remains of a Roman house with its mosaic floor. There are convincing reconstructions including a Roman market place and the kitchen of a Roman house along with an interactive display on Roman technology. There is also an opportunity to handle genuine artefacts.

Canterbury Tales, The 3E 5

St Margaret's Street. Tel: 01227 479227.
Within the historic interior of St. Margaret's Church, the visitor is transported back to the 14th century,

Canterbury Westgate Towers

St. Peters Street. Originally part of the city walls and one time a prison, the Westgate Towers have resolutely stood guard over the road from London since 1380. The arch beneath the towers, once used by pilgrims visiting the tomb of Thomas Becket still allows traffic through, but of a different, motorised kind.

Great Stour and Westgate Towers

with all its sights, sounds and smells to join Chaucer's famous pilgrimage from London to Canterbury and meet the writer himself and his fellow pilgrims. Audio guides relate stories of love and romance, mixed with those of trickery, bawdiness and death as the Knight, The Miller, the Wife of Bath, the Nun's Priest and the Pardoner tell their tales. Finally the pilgrims reach their destination and experience Canterbury's medieval market place and a recreation of the shrine of St. Thomas Becket in Canterbury Cathedral.

Dane John Mound
6C **4**

Castle Row.
Once the site of a Roman burial ground, the Dane John Mound later formed part of a Norman motte and bailey castle. James Simmons, a Canterbury Alderman, remodelled the site in the 18th century with the addition of the Dane John gardens, the walkway to the summit, and the obelisk.

Druidstone Park
1A **38**

Honey Hill, Blean.
Tel: 01227 765168.
Druidstone is for all ages, set in gardens and ancient woodlands. There is a farmyard with friendly animals, adventure play areas, a themed trail through the enchanted woods where there are bluebells in spring

and an ever changing collection of trees and shrubs through the summer season.

Ducking Stool, The
2D **4**

The Old Weavers Restaurant Garden, St Peters St. Dating from Medieval times, and involving a submersion in the River Stour, this device had many uses: firstly as a deterrent and humiliation to an argumentative woman or nagging wife; secondly as a punishment for cheating businessmen following which they were forced from the city, and thirdly, and most notoriously, as a test for witches. If after having been "ducked", the victim lived, they were thus "proven" to be a witch and then burned, if they died, they were innocent and were given a Christian burial.

Eastbridge Hospital
2D **4**

25 High Street. Tel: 01227 47168.
Built in the 12th century, Eastbridge Hospital of St Thomas the Martyr originally offered a temporary home to the less well off pilgrims visiting the shrine of Thomas Becket in the Cathedral. For the last 400 years it has offered permanent hospitality to the elderly as almshouses. On view to the visitor are the undercroft where the original pilgrims found shelter, the refectory which contains an early 13th century mural, and two chapels where services are still held.

Fordwich Town Hall
4E 41

King Street, Fordwich.
Fordwich lays claim to being the smallest town in Britain and in it stands allegedly the smallest Town Hall in Britain still in use. Built in 1544 and originally thatched, the Hall has a maximum capacity of just over 40 people, yet in its time has been the town jail and courthouse. It contains the town Ducking Stool and has a small room in which the nagging wives and argumentative women who fell victim to a "ducking" dried out. Also on display are the town drums, used to warn the town of possible danger and the muniment chest, holding town records, believed to be 800 years old.

Greyfriars Chapel (remains of)
3C 4

off Stour Street. Tel: 01227 471688
(Eastbridge Hospital).
Straddling the River Stour stands this little building, the last remnant of the first English Franciscan Friary. Built in the early years of the 13th century, Greyfriars grew to become a sizeable and important monastery, but during the Suppression under Henry VIII, it was dissolved and the friars ejected. Only this fragment remains consisting of an exhibition area on the ground floor explaining the history of the monastery, and a working chapel above. Outside the building is a small walled garden, an oasis of peace in the midst of a busy city.

Howletts Wild Animal Park
3H 45

Bekesbourne Lane, Bekesbourne.
Tel: 0844 842 4647.
Set in 90 acres of Kentish countryside, Howletts was originally a private zoo for the late John Aspinell but since opening to the public in 1975 it has become a well respected centre of wildlife conservation. All the animals here are threatened with extinction in their natural environment. The aim is to breed and return them to protected areas within their homelands. There are tigers within glass fronted enclosures, leopards, monkeys, rhinos, a walk-through Lemur enclosure, wolves, deer, the largest group of Western Lowland gorillas in the world, elephants, tree shrews and a host of others. The Education Centre describes conservation work abroad.

Norman Staircase
1G 5

The King's School, The Borough.
Built about 1160, the Norman Staircase formerly led to a lodging house for pilgrims on their way to the Cathedral; it is now the entrance to King's School Library. During World War II, the staircase suffered minor damage from flying debris and has subsequently been restored.

Quenin Gate (Remains)
2H 5

Set in the city wall near Broad Street, remnants of Roman brick work and masonry blocks are preserved in the arch of the gateway that leads to the Cathedral buildings

Sir John Boy's House
1E 5

28 Palace Street.
Noted for its disturbing lean and believed to have been built by Sir John Boys M.P. and Recorder of Canterbury, there is some contention as to the precise history of this building; however, it is known to date from the early 1600's. In more recent times, The King's School shop traded from here. It allegedly became crooked following alterations to a chimney.

St Augustine's Abbey & Museum EH
2G 43

Longport. Tel: 01227 378100.
Shortly after the missionary Augustine was sent by the Pope to establish Christianity in Britain in 597 AD, he set about building a monastery outside the city walls and a Cathedral within. St Augustine's Abbey, as it is now known, flourished and was particularly famous for the illuminated manuscripts produced within its scriptorium which became well known throughout the Christian world. Following the Norman conquest, the Abbey was largely rebuilt in the Romanesque style and a Norman abbot installed. The Dissolution of the Monasteries under Henry VIII saw the closure and systematic destruction of the majority of the Abbey with Henry himself converting part of it into a palace which survived until a great storm in 1703. Today, the ruins, whilst not substantial, are part of the Canterbury World Heritage Site and have a museum containing decorative stonework and other items found on the site, and an audio tour is available.

St Dunstan's Church
1E 43

St Dunstans Street.
A small church, founded at the end of the 11th century with important historical connections. It was here in 1174 that Henry II, making a penitential pilgrimage for the murder of Archbishop Thomas Becket changed from royal clothing into sackcloth and walked to Becket's tomb in Canterbury Cathedral. The church also allegedly holds the severed head of Sir Thomas More, Lord Chancellor to Henry VIII. Having been executed for refusing to accept Henry as head of the new Church of England, his daughter claimed his head and it was buried with her in the vault of her husband. Following the canonisation of Sir Thomas by the catholic church in 1935, St Nicholas Chapel, directly above the vault, has become a place of pilgrimage.

St George's Tower
4F 5

St George's Street.
The only remnant of the large church of St. George the Martyr, "The Clock Tower" as it is locally known was bombed during the "Baedeker Raids" of 1942, the church itself being gutted and later demolished. The clock survived and was restored in 1955. Now bereft of its nave and chancel, the tower has a plaque stating that the Elizabethan dramatist Christopher Marlowe was baptised in the church in 1564.

St Martin's Church
2H 43

North Holmes Road.
Tel: 01227 768072 (Church Office).
Forming part of the Canterbury World Heritage Site, St Martin's is the oldest church in England still in use, dating from the 6th century or earlier. It was the chapel used by the Christian Queen Bertha, wife of the Anglo Saxon King Ethelbert, and forms part of the church seen today. When Augustine was sent from Rome to preach the Christian message to the English people, it too became his place of worship. Additions were made between the 7th and 14th centuries including a reworked nave, the chancel and tower

and a restoration was undertaken in the 19th century. Outside in the churchyard is the grave of Mary Tourtel, the creator of Rupert Bear.

St Mary Magdalene's Tower
3G 5

Burgate.
In the middle of the Burgate shopping precinct stands all that remains of the medieval church of St Mary Magdalene. In 1681 the neighbouring parish of St George was joined with that of St Mary and over time the church of the latter fell into disrepair, being finally demolished in 1871; the tower however remained and holds a relocated Baroque memorial to John Whitfield, a local benefactor. In part of the nave of the old church is a garden area. Ironically, all that remains of the church of St George is its tower, the rest being badly damaged in the war and later demolished.

Tower House
1B 4

Westgate Gardens, off St Peter's Place.
Once the home of Catherine Williams, Canterbury's first female mayor, and now used as the Lord Mayor's office and for official functions.

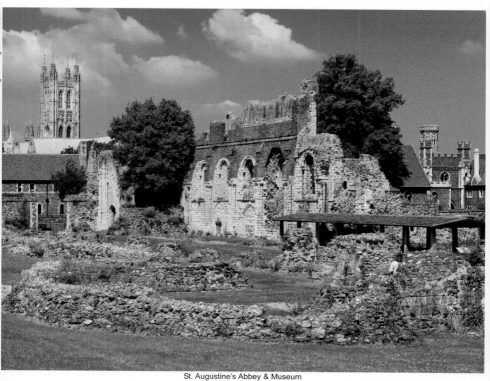

St. Augustine's Abbey & Museum

Chart Gunpowder Mills 4D **46**
18th century explosives mill.
Off Stonebridge Way, Faversham.
Tel: 01795 534542 (Fleur de Lis Heritage Centre).

Crampton Tower Museum 3G **29**
Small museum set in original waterworks
showcasing the work of English engineer Thomas
Crampton.
The Broadway, Broadstairs, CT10 2AB.
Tel: 01843 871133.

Dickens House Museum 3H **29**
Commemorates the novelist's association with
Broadstairs. Dickens memorabilia prints, costume
and Victoriana.
2 Victoria Parade, Broadstairs, CT10 1QS.
Tel: 01843 861232.

Drapers Windmill 4A **12** Restored smock mill
built in 1845. Small museum displays 18th and 19th
century milling artefacts.
St Peters Footpath (off College Rd), Margate,
CT9 2SP. Tel: 01843 291696.

Droit House 2F **7** Droit House houses the Thanet
Visitors Information Centre.
The Stone Pier, Margate, CT91HB.
Tel: 01843 577577.

East Northdown Farm Gardens 4E **13** Farmhouse
gardens with many rare 'Mediterranean' plants. Plant
Nursery and Garden Centre.
East Northdown, Margate, CT9 3TS.
Tel: 01843 862060.

Faversham Stone Chapel EH 4A **46** Ruins of the
small Anglo-Saxon and medieval chapel.
In field immediately North of A2 just West of
Ospringe and opposite Faversham Road.

Fleur de Lis Heritage Centre 4F **47** Faversham
Museum, incorporating the Fleur de Lis Gallery, is
housed here and provides an insight into the history
of Faversham.
10-13 Preston Street, Faversham, ME13 8NS.
Tel: 01795 590726.

Gazen Salts Nature Reserve 3B **48** 1.5 miles of
winding paths guiding visitors through the 15 acre
man made nature reserve.
Richborough Road / Strand Street, Sandwich.

Herne Bay Museum & Gallery 2D **18** History of
the Victorian seaside resort of Herne Bay and its
surrounding area.
12 William Street, Herne Bay, CT6 5EJ.
Tel: 01227 367368.

Herne Windmill 5E **19** Restored Kentish smock
mill. Mill Lane, Herne Bay, CT6 7DR.

Maison Dieu EH 5C **46** Flint and timber-framed
building displaying Roman artefacts from nearby
sites.
West corner of Water Lane in village of
Ospringe, Faversham.Tel: 01795 534542.

Margate Shell Grotto 3H **7** Made of 4.6 million
shells, 2000 square feet of mosaic and one big
mystery.
33 Grotto Hill, Margate, CT9 2BU.
Tel: 01843 220008.

Minster Abbey 4G **33** The first English monastery
was founded on the Abbey site in 670 AD. Guided
tours available.
Church Street, Minster, CT12 4HF.

Monkton Nature Reserve 1A **32** 16 acres of
woodland, cliffs and chalk grassland set inside an
abandoned chalk quarry.
Monkton, Ramsgate, CT12 4LH.
Tel: 01843 822666.

Oare Gunpowder Works Country Park 2C **46**
Former site of gunpowder industry now transformed
into country park with marked trails through woodland
and grassy glades.
Accessible from Tin Shop Hill off Bysing Wood Road,
Oare, Faversham.
Tel: 01795 417850 (Swale Borough Council).

Oare Meadow Nature Reserve 1D **46** Two hectares
of wet meadow on the edge of Oare village, near
Faversham. Located between the Oare Gunpowder
Works and the head of Oare Creek, near Faversham.
Tel: 01622 662012 (Kent Wildlife Trust).

Pegwell Bay Country Park 6E **35** Forms part of the
Sandwich & Pegwell Bay Local Nature Reserve.
Ramsar Site of International Importance and a great
place to explore.
Accessible from A256/Sandwich Road, near
Sandwich. Tel: 01303 266 327.

Pinball Parlour, The 5A **6** Quirky museum housing
an array of playable pinball machines dating back to
the 1960s.
2 Addington Street, Ramsgate, CT11 9JL.

Powell-Cotton Museum 2F **25** Founded in 1896 to
display natural history specimens and cultural objects
collected on expeditions to Asia and Africa. The
museum now displays a wide range of collections
created by six generations of the Powell-Cotton
family. Quex Park, Birchington, CT7 0BH.

Reculver Towers and Roman Fort, Reculver Country Park

Quex Park 2F **25** Unique 250 acre country park consisting of many attractions that include Quex House and Gardens, Powell-Cotton Museum, Jungle Jims soft play area, Quex Craft Village, Quex Falconry Centre and many more.
Park Lane, Birchington, CT7 0BH.

RAF Manston History Museum 5C **26** Museum based on the history of the famous airfield from 1916 to the present day.
Manston Road, Ramsgate, CT12 5DF.
Tel: 01843 825224

Reculver Country Park 1D **20** 37 hectares of meadow and grassland with stunning sea views, picnic areas and a visitor centre. Managed by Kent Wildlife Trust.
Accessible from Reculver Lane, Reculver, Herne Bay. Tel: 01227 862187 (Reculver Visitor Centre).

Richborough Roman Fort & Amphitheatre EH 1A **48** Extensive remains of the Roman Township at Richborough.
Accessible from Richborough Road, Richborough, Sandwich. Tel: 01304 612013.

Sandwich Guildhall Museum 4B **48** Museum recounting the story of Sandwich from early medieval times.
Cattle Market, Sandwich,CT13 9AH.
Tel: 01304 617197.

Sandwich & Pegwell Bay National Nature Reserve 6E **35** Site of international importance for its waders and wildfowl.
Accessible from Sandwich Road, Cliffsend, Ramsgate. Tel: 01622 662012 (Kent Wildlife Trust).

Secret Gardens of Sandwich, The 4C **48** Lutyens-Jekyll designed garden positioned within the heart of Sandwich. Tea rooms. The Salutation, Knightrider Street, Sandwich, CT13 9EW. Tel: 0 1304 619919.

Shepherd Neame Brewery 4F **47** Guided tours through this busy working brewery to see how beer is made from barley. Booking advised, see www.shepherd-neame.co.uk.
The Visitor Centre, 11 Court Street, Faversham, ME13 7AX. Tel: 01795 542016.

Snappys Adventure Play 6A **16** Large indoor adventure playground with play area for under 4s.
45b Joseph Wilson Industrial Estate, Millstrood Road, Whitstable, CT5 3PS. Tel: 01227 282100.

Spitfire & Hurricane Memorial Museum 5C **26** Memorial museum commemorating the Battle of Britain. Two fine examples of the Spitfire and Hurricane fighter aircraft, artefacts, memorial tapestry and garden.
RAF Manston, Manston Road, Ramsgate, CT12 5DF. Tel: 01843 821940.

St. Augustine's Cross EH 4E **35** 19th century cross of Saxon design marking the traditional site of St. Augustine's landing on the shores of England in 597 AD.
Accessible from Cottington Road, Cliffsend, near Ramsgate.

St Peter's Church, Sandwich 4C **48** Church of Norman origin. Permanent display about the Earls of Sandwich is sited at the west end of the church.
St Peter's Street, Sandwich, CT13 9DA.
Tel: 01304 614390.

Seafront houses at Whitstable

Turner Contemporary 1F **7**
A landmark seafront art gallery opened in 2011 to both celebrate JMW Turner's link with Margate and mount interesting temporary exhibitions and events. Rendezvous, Margate, CT9 1HG. Tel: 01843 233000.

Viking Ship (Hugin) 4G **35** Replica of a viking ship that sailed from Denmark to Thanet in 1949 on permanent display on the cliff top at Pegwell Bay. External viewing only. Pegwell Bay, Ramsgate. Tel: 01843 577577.

Walley World 3G **11** Children's indoor adventure playground. 18-21 Marine Terrace, Margate, CT9 1XJ. Tel: 01843 298752.

Walpole Bay Hotel & Museum 2B **12** 1920's hotel and living museum. Original oil lamps, trellis gated Otis lift, original toaster and much more. Fifth Avenue, Cliftonville, Margate, CT9 2JJ. Tel: 01843 221703.

White Mill Rural Heritage Centre 3A **48** 18th century smock windmill with original wooden machinery plus millers cottage and craft museum. The Causeway, Ash Road, Sandwich, CT13 9JB. Tel: 01304 239544.

Whitstable Oyster Yawl 'Favourite' 3E **15** Built in 1890 by the Whitstable Shipping Company and in working order until 1944, this is the last Oyster Yawl to remain in Whitstable and in public ownership. Now a much loved part of the street scene in Island Wall. Island Wall, Whitstable.

Whitstable Museum & Gallery 4F **15** Depicts Whitstable's seafaring traditions through fascinating displays with special features on oysters, diving and shipping. 5a Oxford Street, Whitstable, CT5 1DB. Tel: 01227 276998.

SAFETY CAMERA INFORMATION

PocketGPSWorld.com's CamerAlert is a self-contained speed and red light camera warning system for SatNavs and Android or Apple iOS smartphones/tablets. Visit www.cameralert.co.uk to download.

Safety camera locations are publicised by the Safer Roads Partnership which operates them in order to encourage drivers to comply with speed limits at these sites. It is the driver's absolute responsibility to be aware of and to adhere to speed limits at all times.

By showing this safety camera information it is the intention of Geographers' A-Z Map Company Ltd., to encourage safe driving and greater awareness of speed limits and vehicle speed. Data accurate at time of printing.